MW01101021

It's All in Timing

Jagdish C. Maheshri, Ph.D.

It's All in Timing

Jagdish C. Maheshri, Ph.D.

Noble House

Baltimore, Maryland

It's All in Timing

Library of Congress
Cataloging in Publication Data
ISBN 1-56167-353-6

Library of Congress Card Catalog Number:
97-065522

Published by

8019 Belair Road, Suite 10
Baltimore, Maryland 21236

Manufactured in the United States of America

Acknowledgments

The following people are responsible for making this work a reality:

My wife, Pushpa, and children who had to put up with my whims, yet they wholeheartedly supported my efforts.

My editor, Kimberly Barker, for her invaluable help in tremendously improving the clarity of the material in this book.

And my loving brothers, sister, and my uncle Shantikaka for their continuous encouragement and much needed moral support.

To Bai (my late mother)
in spirit, who has always been with me,
without her love and inspiration this work
wouldn't be possible.

Table of Contents

1. Introduction

Most of us have always been curious about our fate, destiny, and future happenings, especially those of us who have gone through unexpected times of turbulence and despair for which often there is no rational explanation. These experiences shatter our security, a state, as living creatures, we always strive for. And thus, when we recognize our vulnerability to situations beyond our control, we tend to take refuge in anything that offers us hope to regain the feeling of security and stability.

A lot of people easily despair when they meet unexpected situations and cannot cope with them. Some are driven to severe depression, losing control of their lives since they just can't understand "why them?" Others who are perhaps a bit optimistic turn to religion to seek refuge; while still others look for those who could help them understand why they are surrounded with certain unique and undesirable experiences putting them through a very difficult time.

Interestingly, sooner or later, most of these people somehow do survive, although their lives now are transformed to a different level or phase or setting in their lives. Having lived through these experiences they start believing in destiny, fate, and external mystic forces affecting their lives. As a result, it is no surprise that some of us are very curious about what lies in our future and seek consultations from people who can help: psychics, astrologers, and the like.

Astrology has been around for a long, long time. During the ancient period of Greek and Indian civilizations it was extremely popular. Astrologers were well respected. Today astrology doesn't quite enjoy that status for a variety of reasons. For one, with the advent of scientific progress and development over the last several centuries, for any science to survive its basis must be tested and verified. Astrology, unfortunately, over these years has been neglected as a thing of the past and labeled as a satanic practice. Apparently it is perceived as a negative force that causes one to lose control over his life. As a result, it has primarily remained in the hands of those who are unable to treat and respect it as a science. It never had a chance to bloom and to further develop based on research. Thus, mostly it remains mired in skepticism with its orthodoxy tinged. So it's not surprising that the popularity of astrology has become limited to just a passing interest, and at least on the surface, it has been ridiculed and made fun of, perhaps by the very people who are dying to know what lies ahead in their futures.

In my opinion, one of the biggest obstacles keeping astrology from universal acceptance is its very nature of *affecting* an individual. Assuming it is reasonably perfected as a science for making future predictions, it is very easy for a normal individual to become overwhelmed with it to the extent that the individual loses control of his or her life by literally becoming a slave of astrology. But if the very same individual looks at astrology as a guide or means to understand unique happenings surrounding him in his life, astrology becomes a blessing. It allows a person to enrich and enhance his life by helping uncover his hidden talents and abilities, it further helps him discover who he or she is, and even helps provide meaning to life.

What I'm fascinated with most about astrology is the possibilities it offers at the collective human experience level. It has the ability to foresee the steps of human evolution. For instance, the exponential technological growth that has occurred in this century certainly affects the way we live today. From a global evolution standpoint, we as human beings definitely have been transformed to a different (and perhaps a much higher) level during this century. The rapid evolutionary growth can be convincingly explained perhaps only through astrology by understanding the influence of planetary motions on our collective human conscious. Further, with the aid of astrology, the future of human evolution can be predicted, and to some extent, it can provide us the opportunities to avoid pitfalls and use our energies in a positive and harmonious manner to realize the full growth of our collective human conscious.

On one May afternoon in the late sixties in India I accidentally ran into my (distant) uncle, Shantikaka ("Shanti" is his name, and "kaka" means uncle in my mother tongue) who is more like a friend to me than an uncle. He was on his way to attend a lecture by a well known astrologer. He pretty much dragged me along. This was my first exposure to astrology. Honestly, I wasn't impressed by the lecturer. But it was after the lecture when the lecturer uttered the word "solid geometry" to a few of us (when my uncle was waiting for his turn to inquire about meeting the astrologer personally) that my curiosity was aroused. Perhaps I wouldn't have become interested in astrology and been writing this book if it weren't for this incident. He was telling the people surrounding him how important it is to know the principles of solid geometry, in particular, pertaining to the three dimensional celestial space. Those were my college days, and I just had completed a course in solid geometry. My curiosity was aroused. So I bought his books to find out how solid geometry is used in astrology. To my dismay, I did not find a whole lot about solid geometry applications in his books. But some of the things that I read in those books were so ridiculous to me that I took it as a personal challenge to prove them wrong. I ended up doing a lot of reading and research. The more I tried to challenge rules (the logic of interpreting a planetary configuration for predicting an event) the deeper I got into the mess. Although I discovered many rules that resulted in unsuccessful application, the very questioning of those rules forced me to seek solutions elsewhere.

The next several years I continued my pursuit as time permitted. I analyzed thousands of horoscopes. In the beginning it was a hobby. Soon it turned into a profession. With the use of a computer, I figured out a way to compute the geocentric positions of the planets. Later, in the early eighties, using my personal computer my program would print out a horoscope in less than 30 seconds. That was a big step! I was no longer spending 30 to 45 minutes to manually cast a horoscope. I could now devote more time for research on analyzing and interpreting a horoscope. I was improving and using unique approaches in interpreting a horoscope with fairly good accuracy. But when it came to timing a prediction, an important step of astrology, there were cases that would defy the prediction logic which I thought was unchallengable! I wasn't very happy with the methods of timing a prediction with a reasonable degree of accuracy.

It was not until the early nineties that I accidentally discovered a new approach. This approach has totally revolutionized the way to time a prediction, as was dramatically reflected in my confidence and success rate.

My intention behind publishing this book is, therefore, twofold. First, I have noticed that there isn't a really good book written in English that gives comprehensive information on eastern approaches (particularly those from India) to Astrology. I hope this book will provide a starting point for a western astrologer or a Westerner interested in astrology. Secondly, before I explain my unique approach of timing a prediction, a reader who is not familiar with astrology needs some background information and the techniques employed in analyzing and interpreting a chart. With that in mind, I have divided the book in two parts. In the first, I have attempted to cover the "What and How?" portion of astrology, focusing more on the eastern approach. The "When?" part, which is the main driving force behind this writing, is covered in the second part.

Briefly, the first part contains eight sections (or chapters). In the second section, our solar system's astrological significance is covered. The successive sections describe the zodiac, the houses in a horoscope, the horoscope casting procedures, and the house-planet connections. As an example, the late former president Mr. Richard Nixon's horoscope is used for illustrating the horoscope casting process. The material covered in these sections is basically reference material for applying a fixed zodiac based approach of eastern astrology. In these sections I have attempted to include the basic information required to get started. For a serious reader or researcher in astrology I strongly recommend the books listed in the bibliography. They provide detailed basic information on eastern astrology.

The eighth section demonstrates the horoscope analysis and interpretation technique. Mr. Nixon's horoscope is again used. The last section presents the concept of the "ninefold horoscope" of a birth chart.

In the second part, the planetary cycles are described. The heart of the "When?" part is explained by applying my unique Ninefold Progression technique. It's my intention and hope that with the aid of this book, and with a little patience and practice, a reader unfamiliar with astrology should be able to apply the simple technique of "Ninefold Progression." I sincerely hope the reader finds this book a fun and a rewarding experience!

Finally, you are completely mislead if this book makes you believe that astrology will solve all your personal problems. It's my belief that you can benefit from astrology only when you consider it as a means of personal guidance, a source of second opinion, or a way of confirming things that you already had planned. Do not ever let astrology control your life!

Part I: What and How?

2. Our Solar System—The Sun and the Planets

Our solar system consists of the Sun and the planets orbiting around the Sun. The motion of these planets is a result of the gravitational pull exerted by each of these planets due to others as well as due to the Sun. The orbital trajectory of each of these planets around the Sun is an ellipse with the Sun being located at one of the foci of the ellipse.

The motion of a planet in its orbit, as discovered by Kepler, is such that it traces an equal area as part of the elliptical orbit in an equal interval of time. In other words, as the planet, while moving in its orbit, gets closer to the Sun it moves at a faster speed to compensate for the smaller portion of the elliptical orbit it's tracing and, likewise, it slows down in its orbit as it starts moving away from the Sun. Another important characteristic of a planet's motion is that the square of its period of revolution around the Sun is proportional to the cube of its mean distance from the Sun. For example, Saturn is a slower moving planet compared to Mars because Saturn is farther away from the Sun as compared to Mars from the Sun. Likewise, Saturn is a faster moving planet compared to Uranus, as the latter is even farther away from the Sun.

We have nine known planets in our solar system. While the planets Mercury and Venus, being closer to the Sun than our Earth to the Sun, are referred as internal planets; the planets Mars, Jupiter, Saturn, Uranus, Neptune, and Pluto are called external planets.

Later we'll see how astrologically the motion and a particular configuration of the position of the Sun and these planets in the space around us (the Earth) affect us individually as well as collectively. In addition, we'll examine how certain other bodies in space around the earth, real as well as fictitious, affect us.

One of them is our Earth's satellite, the Moon. Her effect is significant because of her proximity. The effects of the moons of other planets (like Jupiter's moons) on us are implicitly lumped with the effect of the moons' parent planets. Thus, the effects of Jupiter's moons are already accounted in the astrological characteristics of the planet Jupiter.

The points of intersection of the plane of the ecliptic (the Earth's orbital plane around the Sun) with the Moon's orbital plane around the Earth often seem to have a great deal of influence on us. These fictitious planets lay exactly opposite of each other as seen from the Earth. In ephemeris they are referred as ascending and descending nodes of the Moon. They are also called the "Dragon's head" or Rahu and the "Dragon's tail" or Ketu. In subsequent discussions we will refer to these lunar nodes as the Rahu and Ketu.

Thus, the influence of the Sun, two interior planets, six exterior planets, the Moon, and Rahu and Ketu are included in our astrological analysis. Their influence depends upon their unique positions in the space around the Earth as seen from the earth (astronomically it is referred to as the Geocentric system) as well as their apparent motion as observed from the Earth. While the planets always move in the forward direction in their orbits with respect to the Sun, planets sometimes appear to be moving backward or retrograde when seen from the Earth. The phenomena of retrograde motion is due to the fact that when a planet orbiting around the

Sun moves with an angular speed slower than that of the Earth around the Sun it appears to move backward in the sky as seen from the Earth. An exterior planet becomes retrograde in its motion when the Earth is in between the planet and the Sun. For an interior planet, however, its retrograde motion becomes apparent when it lies between the Sun and the Earth. The astrological significance of a retrograde planet is discussed in Section 8, "Analysis/Interpretation" of a horoscope.

The astrological significance of the planets and the Sun are summarized below. Although the Sun is not a planet, for astrological purposes the term "planet" here includes the Sun along with other planets. Keep in mind that the influence of the planets on an individual is the sum total of varying degrees of planetary effects due to their mutual orientation, inter-aspects, the zodiac signs they occupy, and the houses they reside in. These factors and their interpretations will become apparent later in successive chapters. The intent here is to familiarize the reader with some general characteristics of individual planets from the astrological standpoint. For brevity, the description provided here is in the form of nouns and adjectives that describe their characteristics.

Sun

Life force, life spirit, soul, life energy, creativity, pursuit of knowledge, vitality, inspiration, dignity, self-esteem, self-discipline, body immune system, alertness, power of senses, health.

Confident, constructive, positive, righteous, just, proud, strong willed, ambitious, royal, noble, optimist, bold, brilliant, powerful, authoritative, generous, gracious, vigorous, warm, masculine, influential, king, leader, commander.

Success, fame, universal love.

Lion, Horse, Boar, Swan.

Sundays, East, mountains, government buildings, public offices, orange color, gold, father, son.

Moon

Sensitive, emotional, beautiful, receptive, compassionate, moody, restless, vascillating, timid, transient, feminine.

Childhood, conception, embryo, infants, family life, home, personal and private affairs, mother, society, social functions.

Water, lakes, ponds, rivers, bays, oceans, aquatic animals, milk, honey, liquids, pearls, perfumes, flowers, fruits, vegetables, dairy products, agriculture products, fishery, breweries, sugar, cooked food, stomach, digestive system, uterus, ovaries, bladder.

Mondays, white color, silver.

Mars

Fierce, masculine, energetic, ambitious, courageous, forceful, dominating, fighter, soldier, aggressive, short tempered, very independent, violent, animal, impulsive, gambler, sportsman, leader, resourceful, generous, noble, adventurous, hardworking, stubborn, confident, executioner, selfish, self-centered, proud.

Revenge, resistance, competition, fights, success, never easily gives up, big ego, machismo, anger.

People in military, army, navy, and air force, captain, general, farmers, butchers, barbers, thieves, robbers.

Blood, fire, burns, hot summer months, fever, sharp weapons, body heat, bleeding, murders, killing, being attacked by cruel animals, accidents, fine by the law, poison, authority, ammunition, copper, engineering, chemistry, chemicals, surgery, medicine, mathematics.

Tuesdays, red color, body nervous system.

Mercury

Pragmatic, practical, political, shrewd, witty, clever, street smart, talkative, smiling, unsure, vascillating, neutral, student, mischievous, humorous, boastful, liar, adaptive, loves brain teasers, appears younger than his (or her) age.

Mind, brain, knowledge, basic education, memory, presence of mind, voice, speech, observation, curiosity, deductive reasoning, analytical mind, short term plans, basic intelligence, good grasping power and capacity.

A large circle of friends, younger kin, fond of children, relations, particularly uncles, books, printing press, journalism, literature, grammar.

Salespersons, accountants, arithmeticians, businessmen, economists, insurance agents, speech writers, publishers, newspaper editors, reporters, writers, orators, narrators, linguists, typists, comedians, lawyers, undercover detectives, jack of all trades.

Wednesdays, green color.

Venus

Feminine, social, extrovert, graceful, attractive, affectionate, gentle, sympathetic, kind, loving, harmonious, sensuous, well mannered, fashionable, sweet voice, pleasant smile, curly hair, and magical eyes; pursues material things to fully enjoy the life, understanding, emotional.

Marriage, weddings, relationships, love affairs, sexual pleasures, material pleasures, wealth, money, estate, prosperity, richness.

Cars, movies, cinema, theaters, entertainment, jewelry, perfumes, cosmetics, diamonds, gems, flowers, spring season, milk, juicy and tasty fruits, textile, silk, restaurants.

Poets, musicians, singers, artists, actors, dancers, magicians.

Fridays, all shades of blue color as well as mixed and match colors, eyes, chin, reproductive system.

Jupiter

Masculine, modest, righteous, just, noble, honest, sincere, law abiding, moral, virtuous, progressive, prosperous, peace loving, respected, generous, optimist, auspicious, religious, unselfish, happy, spiritual, self-esteemed, quiet.

Good conduct, reputation, faith, high ideals, wisdom, knowledge, education, teaching, philosophy, long term perspective, expansion.

Schools, colleges, universities, educational institutes, research institutes, charitable nonprofit institutions, temples, churches, mosques, synagogues, courts, assembly halls.

Preacher, religious leader, teacher, student, a true learner, professor, philosopher, novelist, guru.

Wealth, money, fortune, social prestige, fame, popularity, recognition, success, respect, family life, happiness from children.

Thursdays, yellow color, body fat.

Saturn

Slow, lazy, rotten, dirty, miser, rejected, cold, handicapped, dull, binding, defensive, nervous, disharmonious, patient, prudent, wise, industrious, sincere, conservative, introvert, very quiet, laconic, practical, pessimist, thoughtful, worrisome, shrewd, careful, long term planner, serious, restrictive.

Darkness, misfortune, secrecy, hardship, loss, longevity, death, delays, old age, poverty, problems, obstructions, sorrow, unhappiness, mourning, destruction, shrinkage, toughness, unlucky, lifeless, dust, renunciation of material things, limitations, denial, disappointment, dispute, difficulty, obstacles, hindrances, differences, plodding, perseverance, savings, endurance, thrift, self control, sense of duty, concentration, meditation, prayers, calculative, fall, negotiations.

Chronic illness, bones, rheumatism, tuberculosis, leprosy, paralysis, muteness.

Thin built, slender, bony, pale, older looking for his age, deep set eyes.

Old buildings, slums, leather and shoe factories, slaughter houses, lead, iron, steel, oil, petroleum products, wool, hair, nails, tortoise.

Labor problems, famine, floods, wars, difficult time, depression, loss of material, bankruptcy, lawyers, judges, industrialists, reformers, famous political figures.

Saturdays, black color.

Uranus, Neptune and Pluto were discovered in the last few centuries—Uranus in the 18th century, Neptune in the 19th century, and Pluto in the 20th century. Dane Rudhyar calls them ambassadors of the Galaxy. They act as catalysts for transmitting the influence of the cosmic power from beyond our solar system. In the light of a dramatic increase in the speed of human evolution in the last few centuries, these planets represent the process of repolarization and universalization of consciousness. As a result, human beings have become increasingly receptive and ready for experiencing the cosmic energies. These planets may be considered "transformers" for the release of intense cosmic energies for human beings to receive. Before their discovery they represented latent possibilities of transforming human consciousness, but since their discovery they have become an integral part of the human consciousness. With the awareness of their existence, their influence on humanity as a whole has become so pronounced that it resulted in the accelerated growth of human evolution as well as of our collective mind.

Uranus

Intelligent, dynamic, speedy, precise, intense, extremely powerful and strong (as a comparison, if the Mercury is wind, the Uranus is a tornado), accurate, revolutionary, fond of change, independent, whimsical, unconventional, unorthodox, fearless, unsteady, moody, arrogant, crazy, unpredictable, secretive, masculine, stubborn, agile, mysterious, intuitive, sudden, drastic, quick, eccentric, ambitious, passionate, selfish, pioneer, strange, new, powerful imagination, accurate logic, deductive reasoning, (the Mercury's knowledge is like a starlit night, the Jupiter's knowledge is a moonlit night, while the Uranus's knowledge is a lightning rod in the night!), inspiration, motivation, big ego, homosexual tendencies, freedom.

Science, technology, modern engineering, high technology, super highway, interactive television, telecommunications, wireless communication, cellular phones, air travel, explosives, nuclear weapons, missiles, uranium, radium, atomic energy, bombs, poisonous gas, x-rays, hypnotism, mesmerism, occult, astrology, modern medicine.

Scientists, research fellows, reformers, liberals, magicians, fanatics.

Divorce, separation, horrible accidents, terrible natural disasters, murders, explosions, arsenals, destruction, electric chair.

Paralysis, hysteria, delusion, electrical shock, central nervous system.

Neptune

Divine, intuitive, dreamy, psychic, magical, extremely sensitive, highly emotional, moody, mentally weak, clairvoyant, spirit, inspirational, imaginative, secretive, cynical, quiet, nervous, possessed, compassionate, inexpressive, feminine, worrisome, lazy, dramatic.

Spiritual experiences, hypnotism, mesmerism, misunderstanding, confusion, illusion, fear, unconditional love, non-attachment.

Drugs, poison, gas plants, aviation, voyages by sea, water, liquor, fisheries, modern hospitals, asylums, sanitariums, prisons, chemical plants, modern ammunitions, modern art, miracles.

Insanity, mental disorder, leprosy, allergy.

Magicians, astrologers, psychics, spiritual teachers, contemporary philosophers, poets, musicians, artists, singers, spies, writers, socialists.

Pluto

Sudden, highly revolutionary, influences human beings on a collective level: tribes, groups, nations and like; masculine, creative, diplomatic, destructive, crazy, whimsical, very secretive, mysterious.

Long journeys.

Modern day discoveries and innovations, specialty chemicals, unsolved mysteries, mysterious murders, explosions, bombing, nuclear weapons, nuclear arsenals, world wars, modern day scandals; big social, political, financial and religious events.

Psychiatrist, psychologist, modern surgeons, contemporary famous people in all walks of life.

Rahu

Both Rahu and Ketu influence an individual most by acting as catalysts. They supply the immense energy to the planets with which they unite (the difference between celestial longitude of a planet and one of the nodes being close to zero) or make angles corresponding to their longitudinal difference being close to a value of a multiple of 30 degrees. Rahu's characteristics, in general, are close to that of Saturn while Ketu's to that of Mars.

Dark, evil, masculine, possessed, lame, handicapped, outcast, liar. When unfavorably positioned in the horoscope it brings down the good influence of a planet with which it is associated and intensifies the bad effects; however, it bestows success, fame, popularity, prestige, wealth, luck, and good times to a person if it is favorably positioned in the person's horoscope.

Shadow, illusion, magical spell, black magic, black power, witchcraft, curse, a chain of bad luck, cruelty, tragedy, gambling, temptation, misfortune, poison, loss of sight, blindness, disease, improper diagnosis of a disease, confusing symptoms related to a disease, downfall, why me? type experiences, failure, destruction, strange happenings, loss of memory, low mentality, adoption.

Paternal grandfather, spiritual force, long travels, fortune, good deeds, road to self discovery.

Black color.

Ketu

Non-materialist, world renouncer, seer, unselfish.

Body scars, hemorrhoids, maternal grandfather.

Finally, the Sun, Mars, Saturn, Uranus, Pluto, Rahu, and Ketu are generally considered malicious planets. Their natural disposition is generally considered to be unfavorable. In addition, Mercury is considered a malicious planet if it is in conjunction with any one or more of the malicious planets. The planets Neptune, Jupiter, Venus, Moon, and Mercury (only if they are not in conjunction with any malicious planet) are generally considered auspicious planets. By nature they are generally favorable.

3. Zodiacs

The Earth, while orbiting the Sun in its elliptical trajectory, also rotates around its North-South axis. The plane of its orbit around the Sun is tilted with the plane of Earth's rotation about its North-South axis by about 23 1/2 degrees as shown in Figure 1. The Earth's rotation around itself is from West to East (eastward) once every 24 hours. As a result, the Sun appears to rise in the East in the morning and set in the West in the evening. When observed through successive nights, the stars in the sky will appear to move from East to West.

The spherical space around the Earth (at any time we see only a part of it) is called the celestial sphere. If we extend the Earth's North-South axis into the space in both directions, the points where it meets the horizons are referred as the Celestial Poles, North and South respectively. Since the Earth rotates eastward around its axis the celestial sphere appears to move in the opposite direction, the westward. The projection of the Earth's equator on the celestial sphere is called the Celestial Equator. The Celestial Equator divides the space into the Northern and the Southern hemispheres.

The lines perpendicular to the Celestial Equator passing through the Celestial Poles are the circles. These circles are the projections of the Meridians or Meridian circles on the celestial sphere (Meridians are the imaginary lines forming circles on the Earth's surface drawn perpendicular to the Equator passing through the North and South poles of the Earth). These projected Meridian circles on the celestial sphere are called Declination Circles.

As the Earth orbits around the Sun in its elliptical trajectory once every year, the Sun slowly appears to move from South of the Celestial Equator towards North in the Northern Hemisphere in the early part of the year (January through March). As the Sun crosses the Celestial Equator on about March 21, marking the beginning of the Spring in the Northern Hemisphere and the Fall in the Southern Hemisphere, the day and night become equal in duration (12 hours each) all over the world. On this day the Sun is said to be at the Vernal Equinox, the point at which the Sun crosses the Celestial Equator in the northward direction.

For the next three months the Sun moves northward and reaches its northmost point (about 23 1/2 degrees north of the Celestial Equator) in the sky on about June 21. It is the beginning of Summer in the Northern Hemisphere (and Winter in the Southern Hemisphere), with the maximum hours of daylight on June 21. After June 21, the Sun appears to start its journey southward crossing the Celestial Equator around September 23. The Sun's crossing point across the Celestial Equator as it moves southward is called the Autumnal Equinox. The Autumnal Equinox marks the beginning of the Fall Season in the Northern Hemisphere and Spring in the Southern Hemisphere, and again on this day, the length of day and night become twelve hours each all over the world.

The sun continues its southward journey in the sky until it reaches the southmost point (about 23 1/2 degrees south of the Celestial Equator) on about December 22. Now, the night is longest in the Northern

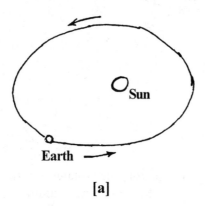

[a]

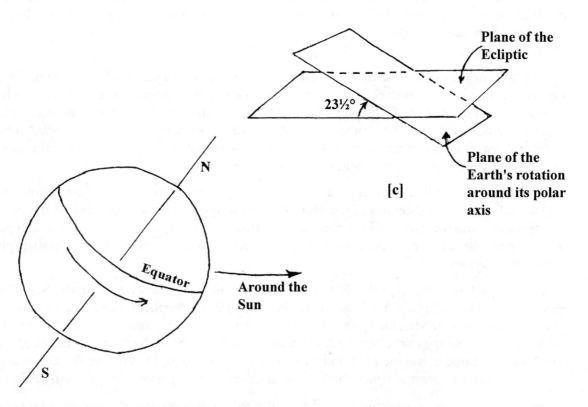

[c]

Earth rotating around its polar axis while orbiting around the Sun.

[b]

—Figure 1—

Hemisphere and it marks the beginning of the Winter Season (while Summer begins in the Southern Hemisphere). After reaching the southmost point, the Sun reverses its course in the sky, resuming its northward journey towards the Celestial Equator. Consequently in the Northern Hemisphere days become longer and nights shorter. Once again on March 21 it crosses the Vernal Equinox, the Sun's northward crossing point of the Celestial Equator.

The Sun's apparent path in the celestial sphere as described above is called the Ecliptic. In other words, the Ecliptic is the projection of the Earth's orbit around the Sun on the celestial sphere. The crossing points of the Ecliptic and the Celestial Equator are called Equinoctial points. Thus, the Vernal Equinox occurs on about March 21 and the Autumnal Equinox on September 23, as the Sun appears at the Equinoctial points on these days. The celestial longitude is the distance measured in one direction (from West to East in the sky and then back to West underneath the Earth around the other side of the Earth) along the Ecliptic from the Vernal Equinox, while the celestial latitude is the distance measured perpendicular to the Ecliptic.

When observed from the Earth, the path along which the planets and the Moon appear to travel in the sky is within a narrow ten degree celestial latitude zone on either side of the Ecliptic. Thus, the band of about 20 degrees latitude zone about the Ecliptic extending in the East-West directions on the celestial sphere is called the zodiac. The zodiac is divided in twelve equal parts of 30 degrees each along the Ecliptic, and the reference or the starting point of the zodiac is the Vernal Equinox. The popular twelve zodiac signs correspond to these twelve equal parts of the zodiac. The daily planetary positions used in astrology today are calculated with the Vernal Equinox as the reference point or zero degrees of Aries.

Although stars do move, their motion is so small compared with the planetary motions, they are considered practically "fixed" in the celestial sphere. Due to the gradual change of orientation, the Earth's polar axis continually wobbles. In the course of time, it points to different pole stars and describes a circle in space in about 26,000 years. Consequently, the positions of the equinoctial points (the Vernal and the Autumnal equinoxes) with respect to the "fixed" stars in the celestial sphere gradually change along the Ecliptic at an annual rate of 50 seconds of arc or at about one degree in 72 years. Thus, the equinoxes return to the same point on the Ecliptic with respect to a fixed star after about 26,000 years. This cycle is called the precession of the equinoxes. This period, divided by 12, gives us the duration for a precessional Age, the current one being the Piscean. The motion of the equinoxes being retrograde, the next Age will be the Aquarian.

As a result of the precession of the equinoxes, the reference point (zero degrees of Aries) of the zodiac (the Vernal Equinox) doesn't remain fixed with respect to a fixed star, but moves along the Ecliptic. In other words, now, at the zero degree of Aries (at the Vernal Equinox) the Sun does not point to the same fixed star as it did at the time of the Spring equinox two thousand years ago. About 2,160 years from now the location of the zero degree of Aries on the Ecliptic will correspond to the location of zero degree of Taurus (the next zodiac sign) today. A zodiac system that bases its reference point to the Vernal Equinox is called the moving zodiac system.

In the West, the moving zodiac system has been widely popular and accepted. However, in the East, particularly in India, the fixed zodiac system has been in use for a very long time. The very basis of the latter system is the eastern premise that the astrological significance of a zodiac sign only depends on its (zodiac sign's) orientation with respect to the "fixed" stars. In other words, the astrological characteristics of a particular location in the zodiac should always be the same since those are defined in relation to the zodiac's specific orientation in the celestial sphere containing the fixed stars.

However, for the fixed zodiac system, the problem arises in establishing the reference point (or the starting point of Aries) on the zodiac. Although there are several reference points (all within a range of four to five degrees) that might be in use today, the most popular and accepted one is based on the star Spica. The star Spica corresponds to the 180 degree location of the fixed zodiac system. The fixed zodiac reference point coincided with that of the moving zodiac reference point about 1700 years ago. In other words, today the zero degree of Aries of the fixed zodiac system corresponds to about 23.75 degrees of Aries of the moving zodiac system. Later it will be shown that the planets occupying the houses in a horoscope are independent of the zodiac system used, and the houses influence an individual far more than the zodiac signs they belong to.

Astrological characteristics attributed to the (twelve) zodiac signs that are in use today are probably the results of thousands of years of experience of astrologers all over the world. Surprisingly, there isn't a great deal of disagreement over these characteristics among astrologers around the world.

Before we get to the characteristics of each zodiac sign, let us briefly look at the groups under which they can be broadly classified. These groups, along with their characteristics are:

Masculine versus Feminine Signs

Starting with Aries all alternate signs are masculine while others are feminine. Thus, Aries, Gemini, Leo, Libra, Sagittarius, and Aquarius are masculine; and Taurus, Cancer, Virgo, Scorpio, Capricorn, and Pisces are feminine.

The masculine signs are physically strong, positive, assertive, active, bold, and offensive in nature. The feminine signs, on the other hand, show a passive, defensive, and a somewhat conciliatory disposition. In general, the feminine signs are physically weak. But they are more compassionate, kind, and human.

Fire, Earth, Air, and Water Signs

This classification of zodiac signs represents their characteristics based on the natural elements: Fire, Earth, Air, and Water. Aries, Leo, and Sagittarius are the fire signs. Taurus, Virgo, and Capricorn are the earth signs. Gemini, Libra, and Aquarius are the air signs; while the water signs are Cancer, Scorpio, and Pisces.

The fire signs are active, assertive, and very independent. They represent a tremendous energy, enthusiasm, and courage. Ambition, strength, daring, dynamism, and eternal optimism are the basic qualities of these signs. They are proud, enterprising, self-confident, and have a natural tendency to lead others than follow them. They love challenges, are generous, and act with full vigor and vitality. They truly represent the essence of life force.

The earth signs are materialistic, possessive, practical, and very business minded. They are very hardworking, productive, a miser to some extent, and always work towards expanding their material wealth and financial stability. In essence, the earth signs are driven by their wants and material needs and will go to any length to achieve their materialistic goal.

The air signs exhibit the nature that clearly distinguishes human beings from animals. They are intelligent, possess very high mental capacity, and from a humanitarian point of view, they provide the true driving force for human evolution. Through their fertile imagination, keen observation, and logical reasoning they truly enjoy the challenges of discovering the mysteries of the universe. They love art, music, and are philosophical. No other signs have done so much for humanity.

The water signs deal with the things that are closer to the heart than the brain. By nature they are very emotional, shy, introverted, a bit timid, sensitive, kind, loving, tender, and touching. Being feminine, they are physically weak, but are emotionally very strong, and they derive their strength through their loving nature. They have a tremendous spiritual power and vivid imagination. No wonder they are psychic!

The following covers the brief description of the individual characteristics of the zodiac signs. Again, please keep in mind that the intent here is to provide readers with a general idea about what these signs signify. For indepth information covering various viewpoints on astrological characteristics of the zodiac signs, one can refer to popular handbooks on astrology, some of which are listed in the bibliography. For brevity, the following description of zodiac sign characteristics is presented in the form of either nouns or adjectives as appropriate.

Aries

Masculine, fierce, animal-like, dynamic, fire, barren, violent, bold, impulsive, rash, combative, independent, energetic, dominating, pushy, moody, ambitious, active, enterprising, deterministic, forceful, impatient, selfish, inconsistent, passionate, arrogant, egoist, stubborn, frank, charming, proud.

Leaders, executives, soldiers, army officers, defense department personnel, surgeons, butchers, barbers, police, law officers, guards, firemen, mechanics, wrestlers, athletes.

Lean masculine body.

Ruled by the planet Mars, a fire sign.

Taurus

Feminine, moist, stable, fixed, earthy, materialistic, possessive, slow but steady, practical, firm, dogmatic, conservative, patient, straightforward, stubborn, strong, selfish, hardworker, disciplined, rainy-day saver.

Actors, singers, musicians, corporations, stockbrokers, bankers, insurance agents, financiers, farmers, jewelers, income tax and sales tax personnel.

Cosmetics, furs, jewels, gems, earrings, watches, agriculture, flowers, mirrors, glass, plastics, ceramics, rubber, milk and dairy products, sugar, vegetables, cattle ranches.

Throat, neck muscles, eyes, broad forehead.

Ruled by Venus, an earth sign.

Gemini

Masculine, barren, plural, twins, human, mentally active, intelligent, indecisive, restless, talented, imaginative, social, loves travel, loves changes, schizophrenic, impulsive, hasty, unsure, anxious, nervous, jack of all trades, worrisome, fond of children, witty, humorous.

Short travel, commerce.

Tall, upright, long hands, thin legs, sharp and active look.

Lungs, cold, bronchitis, tuberculosis.

Writers, journalists, advisors, lawyers, salespersons, bookkeepers, business travelers, postal employees, teachers, professors, photographers, tutors, secretaries, translators, linguists, mediators, orators, engineering contractors, diplomats, merchants, mathematicians.

Schools, nurseries, playhouses, mountains, hills, warehouses, barns.

Ruled by Mercury, an air sign.

Cancer

Emotional, very feminine, dynamic, fruitful, fertile, sensitive, sentimental, psychic, anemic, mute, timid, moody, restless, independent, loyal, mysterious, hospitable, responsible, homesick, family person.

Clumsy body, slender limbs.

Fragile in childhood but health gets better as age advances, chest, stomach, cough, asthma, bronchitis.

Advisors, teachers, historians, antique dealers, restaurant owners, fishermen, sailors, explorers, navigators, navy personnel.

Pearls, dairy products, silver, tea, gasoline, canals, rivers, lakes, shores, cellars, places near water.

Ruled by Moon, a water sign.

Leo

Masculine, hot, dry, animal-like, barren, steady, fixed, noble, energetic, ambitious, famous, graceful, glorious, proud, full of life and vitality, vigorous, aristocratic, majestic, royal, magnanimous, generous, dignified, leader, chief, honorable, strong willed, determined, open, frank, just, fortunate, passionate, cheerful, romantic, attractive.

Managers, authority, kings, captains, presidents, managing directors, government officers, commanders, social workers.

Sports, speculation, pursuit of pleasures, inspiration.

Well developed bones, well built, muscle power, heart, spinal chord, nerves.

Forests, woods, deserts, palaces, castles, mansions, race courses, government buildings, social clubs, casinos, movie halls, theaters, gold mines.

Ruled by Sun, a fire sign.

Virgo

Feminine, barren, cold, dry, materialistic, possessive, intellectual, curious, aware, inconsistent, indecisive, restless, shy, self-conscious, methodical, sensible, pragmatic, rational, practical, down-to-earth, genius, prudent, analytical, good business instincts, mean, cunning.

Slender looking.

Inspectors, detectives, diplomats, teachers, farmers, gardeners, businessmen, accountants, authors, journalists, publishers, editors, ambassadors, artist, actors, comedians.

Ruled by the planet Mercury, an earth sign.

Libra

Masculine, intelligent, dynamic, well informed, logical thinker, mentally active, talented, ambitious, independent, musical, vocal, constructive critic, courteous, gentle, intuitive, pleasant, peace loving, humane, persuasive, instinctive, honest, just, kind, social, generous, liberal.

Tall, well proportioned body, charming, slender, kidneys, spines, uterus.

Photography, drawings, painting, music, art.

Lawyers, judges, artists, actors, musicians, art directors, architects, businessmen.

Cotton, textile, silk, fabrics, wheat, grains, juices.

Ruled by Venus, an air sign.

Scorpio

Violent, feminine, ambitious, imaginative, intimate, moody, depressed, stubborn, dominating, eccentric, sensitive, emotional, determined, dogmatic, outspoken, materialistic, mute, courageous, confident, loves challenges, energetic, resourceful, impulsive, independent, mystical, extremist, impatient, passionate, laconic, blunt, revenge seeker, selfish, forceful, obsessive.

Bladder, womb, ovaries, brain, coma, trance, inflammation, neural disorders.

Chemistry, medicine, maternity, breweries, boilers, steam engines, military, explosives, bombs, sharp weapons, chemicals, acids, poison, chloroform, water supply, beverages, liquors, automobiles, construction, machinery, labor department, horses, elephants, poisonous animals and insects.

Surgeons, dentists, chemists, research workers, detectives, soldiers, planners, money launderers, robbers, burglars, hit men, murderers, killers.

Swamps, drainage areas, slaughter houses, surgical operation rooms, kitchen, gardens, laboratories, meat markets, funeral homes, crematories, incinerators, tanneries.

Ruled by Mars, a water sign.

Sagittarius

Masculine, bold, courageous, ambitious, greedy, self confident, energetic, vigorous, outspoken, just, righteous, religious, sympathetic, intuitive, independent, risk taker, gambler, loves change, likes to travel, philosophical, charming, handsome, graceful, generous.

Tall, well developed body, large forehead.

Hips, thighs, rheumatic pain, lungs.

Teachers, speakers, ministers, archbishops, physicians, politicians, warriors.

Animals, horses, elephants, bow and arrows, spears, swords, poles, needles, sticks, canes, ropes, aquatic animals, fruits, flowers, roots, seeds, medicines.

Ruled by the planet Jupiter, a fire sign.

Capricorn

Materialistic, possessive, feminine, dynamic, animal-like, cold, calculative, businesslike, confident, perseverance, practical, cautious, forceful, ambitious, independent, brave, bold, patient, tolerant, steady, reserved, modest, polite, slow, sincere, reliable, self-centered, diplomatic, tactful, cunning, clever, pessimist, conservative, industrious, skeptical.

Sacrifice, savings, fame, reputation, rules and regulations, solitude, darkness, privacy, secrecy, peace.

Slender, tall, thin and oval shaped face, deep set eyes, coarse hair.

Knees, bones, skin, nails, rheumatism, cold, digestive system.

Businessmen, banking personnel, teachers, mathematicians, philosophers, detectives, physicians, scientists.

Industries, corporations, governments.

Cells, islands, hospitals, asylums, jails, cemeteries, tombs, barren land, cold climate, ancient things, oil, iron.

Ruled by Saturn, an earth sign.

Aquarius

Intelligent, mentally powerful, courteous, artistic, analytical, talented, masculine, fixed, patient, persistent, determined, strong willed, practical, down to earth, pragmatic, self reliant, humane, musical, outspoken, open-minded, impersonal, shrewd, original, individualistic, intuitive, ascetic, lethargic, pessimist, introvert.

Tall, strong, handsome.

Heart, blood pressure.

Modern industries and corporations, high technology, research institutes, artists, scientists, high level diplomats, Nobel laureates.

Meditation, freedom, seclusion.

Ruled by Saturn, an air sign.

Pisces

Feminine, fertile, imaginative, fruitful, weak, timid, sensitive, emotional, inconsistent, indecisive, intimate, dreamy, mute, restless, honest, outspoken, religious, nonviolent, unsteady, polite, modest, moody, affectionate, hermit, psychic, generous, social, kind, unselfish.

Liquid, water, ponds, oceans, lakes, harbor, places near water, liquors, beverages, fantasies, navy, submarines, temples, churches, mosques, synagogues, sanitariums, nursing homes, asylums, jails, prisons, secluded places.

Average height, plump.

Poets, musicians, singers, religious leaders, philosophers, nurses, caterers, social workers, teachers, preachers, saints, actors, sailors, ship captain, fishermen.

Ruled by Jupiter, a water sign.

Planetary Angles

One of the important parts of astrological analysis of a person's chart deals with a careful study of how planets are distributed over the entire band of the zodiac. In essence, the analysis deals with the angles between a planet and all other planets. The following describes the astrological significance of some of the major angles that must be taken into consideration in assessing a planet's overall strength.

An angle between two planets is the smaller difference between their longitudes (positions) measured in degrees. Regardless of the zodiac system used, an angle between two planets remains the same. Thus, the magnitude of an angle can vary from 0° to 180°. Before we discuss the astrological significance for each type of angle, the definition of a pair of planets making a certain angle implies that those planets are with in three degrees of that particular angle. The importance of three degree tolerance will be evident in Section 9 "The Ninefold Horoscope."

Although there are up to 18 different angles an astrologer can take into account, only the major ones will be included in our analysis. They are listed below:

Conjunction (0°): It is favorable between the planets which are complementary in nature with each other. For instance, conjunction of Moon and Jupiter can be very favorable, especially in the ascendant or in the fifth or in the ninth house. Conjunction of Saturn and Sun, however, in most cases, is likely to produce unfavorable results.

Semi-sextile (30°): Relatively it is not that important. Usually, it is considered to be good.

Sextile (60°): It is always favorable between any two planets.

Square (90°): Usually it is considered a bad or unfavorable situation. In my opinion, if both planets are auspicious and respectively placed in favorable houses, the square can turn out to be beneficial. A square (angle) means a challenge! It's up to the individual to get the most out of it.

Trine (120°): It's the most favorable angle between any two planets!

Quincunx (150°): This angle is likely to create a very difficult situation. Overall it is adverse in nature.

Opposition (180°): Good only if both planets are beneficial by nature, or else it's always bad or unfavorable.

4. Horoscope Houses

The basis for astrological predictions for an individual is the particular configuration of the planets as viewed from his (or her) birthplace at the time of his (or her) birth. The form (or format) in which the planetary positions in the space surrounding the place at the time of birth is presented is called a horoscope or a birth chart. Thus, the basic requirement for preparing a person's horoscope is the birth information:

Birth Date
Birth Time
Birth Place

There are different types of formats in use today to describe the planetary positions at a particular time in the space surrounding the place where a person is born. But they all convey the same basic information on which an astrologer bases his predictions.

Incidentally, the meaning of the term "horoscope" as it is being used today is misleading. For example, the "horoscope" we read in the paper today doesn't mean anything that I just described. What we read in the paper today in the horoscope column is a very general prediction provided by an astrologer for all zodiac signs; each corresponding to the zodiac sign occupied by the Sun at the time of birth based on the moving zodiac system. In other countries, particularly in South East Asia where the fixed zodiac system is popular, the similar predictions are based on the zodiac signs either occupied by the Sun or the Moon (the latter being more popular) at the time of birth. However, regardless of the zodiac system used, it is important to recognize that these predictions are based on the effects of only one planet (either the Sun or the Moon) while the effects of other planets are totally ignored. As a result, it's not surprising that most of the time these columns become the target of fun and ridicule as they are inadequate in delivering the individual predictions. In other words, you can't divide the whole world's population in twelve groups and successfully impose the twelve different predictions on them based solely on the Sun or Moon's position in their birth charts.

The horoscope formats that are widely in use today both in the Western (mainly Europe and North America) and Eastern (particularly in India) countries are presented in Figure 4.

The type of horoscope format that is popular in the United States has the appearance of a clock dial as shown in Figure 4 (a) In this chart, the dial is divided in twelve equal parts just like in a clock. These twelve parts are called the "houses" of the horoscope. As it will become apparent later, the configurations of the planets with respect to both the zodiac signs and the houses is unique for every person. This (unique planets-houses combination) is what makes one individual so different from the other with respect to the personality, behavior, and the life experiences that he goes through. In other words, no two horoscopes can be identical as no two human beings are!

The upper half of the Western type horoscope corresponds to what we see in the space above the Earth while the lower one is what is below (other side of the Earth which we cannot see) us. If we stand facing South,

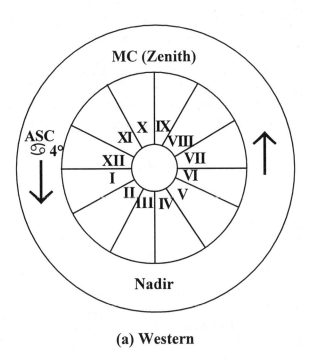

(a) Western

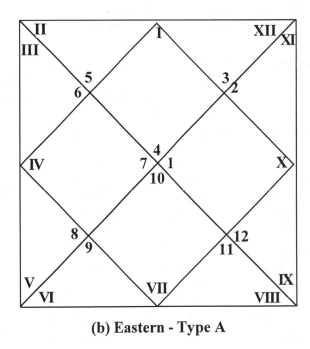

(b) Eastern - Type A

Pisces IX	Aries X	Taurus XI	Gemini XII
Aquarius VIII			Cancer I
Capricorn VIII			Leo II
Sagittarius VI	Scorpio V	Libra IV	Virgo III

(c) Eastern - Type B

Taurus XI / XII Gemini	Aries X	Pisces IX / VIII Aquarius
Cancer I		Capricorn VII
Leo II / III Virgo	IV Libra	Sagittarius VI / V Scorpio

(c) Eastern - Type C

—Figure 4—

the eastern horizon falls on our left and the western horizon on the right. The starting point of the first house or the ascendant begins exactly at the eastern horizon. In the figure, the cusp (the beginning point) of the ascendant is shown to fall in the zodiac sign of Cancer, also called the Cancer rising. In this type of horoscope format, zodiac signs are indicated at the cusps. Cancer being the ascendant, the ascendant cusp is indicated by Cancer 4° at the 9 o'clock location as shown. For avoiding confusion between the zodiac signs and houses, the zodiac signs will be indicated by the number (for Eastern type horoscope formats) and the houses by the Roman numerals. The successive houses then follow along the east-west circle below us (lower half portion of the chart shown in the figure) from one through six. The end of the sixth house which then becomes the starting of the seventh house (or the seventh house cusp) begins exactly at the western horizon. The remaining six houses, seventh through twelfth, trace the upper half of the space (or the visible space) from west to east.

As we described in Section 3, the zodiac is the band of about 20 degree declination that runs parallel to and on both sides of the Ecliptic. This band of zodiac gets mapped in with the space defined as the houses. Thus, the houses in a horoscope are the twelve portions of the east-west circular space (or the zodiac). However, these portions are not necessarily equal with each house containing zodiac length of 30 degrees. The beginning part of a house may correspond to a tail portion of one zodiac sign with the front end part of the next zodiac sign as the remaining portion of the house. Several methods for dividing the zodiac into the houses were proposed, but only a few of them are flawless. With the intent of not losing the focus and sparing readers from intricate mathematical details, the information of the applications of the various proposed methods on the house division and their limitations are not provided here. However, the pertaining references are included in the bibliography. As detailed in the next section, the procedure of casting of a horoscope includes the use of Raphael's tables of houses. The basis for the house division in these tables is the "Semi Arc System" developed by Placidus. This system is universally accepted and popular all over the world.

Depending upon the birthplace and the date of birth, the length of a house may vary from only a 10 degree portion of the zodiac to as high as a 50 degree portion of the zodiac. In other words, while a zodiac sign can be common to two houses, a house may take up to a good portion of two zodiac signs. However, regardless of the birthplace and time, the cusp of a house remains exactly 180 degrees apart from the cusp of its opposite house. Thus, if the cusp of the first house falls on 22 degrees of Aries then the cusp of the seventh house will correspond to 22 degrees of Libra. This will be explained later in detail in the section that describes the procedure of casting of a horoscope.

As described in the figure, in the Western type horoscope, the houses (as indicated with Roman numerals) are always fixed. With the ascendant cusp at the 9 o'clock hour hand position (which will always be at the 9 o'clock position), the first three houses are shown in the lower left quadrant, the next three houses, IV through VI, occupy the lower right corner. The cusp of the fourth house corresponds to the 6 o'clock position. The 6 o'clock position is referred as the Nadir. The houses VI through IX map the upper right quadrant ending with the tenth house cusp at the zenith of the midheaven (also termed as midheaven cusp or MC). The last three houses, houses X through XII, take up the upper left corner space and complete the circle by returning to the ascendant cusp. The Western format of a horoscope seems very logical and straightforward since it directly corresponds to what we see in the sky if we stand facing South with the eastern horizon on our left. The houses VII through XII occupy the visible portion of the space, therefore, the visible planets at a place at the time of the birth reside in one or more of these houses.

In Figure 4, in addition to the Western format, three more formats of a horoscope are illustrated. All the three come from India, and are labeled as the Eastern type A, B, and C. The type A format is the most popular and widely used in the North, West and Central India; the type B is popular in the South, while the type C is very common in the eastern part of India. Notice that in the type A format, just as in the Western horoscope format, the position of the houses shown is always fixed. For the ascendant cusp falling in the sign of Cancer, the number 4 is placed in the first house and the successive zodiac signs are placed in the respective houses with the Gemini (number 3) ending in the twelfth house. Later, while discussing the astrological characteristics of the houses, I will explain why I prefer this particular horoscope format over others. However depending upon the individual preference, any one of these formats will work equally well and there is no reason for anyone not to follow a certain type.

For the eastern type B and C horoscope formats, the zodiac signs have the fixed positions while the houses get positioned according to the rising sign. Thus, for the Cancer rising horoscope, for both of these types, the Roman numeral I is placed in the space labeled for the zodiac sign of Cancer. The successive houses are assigned to corresponding zodiac signs as shown with the twelfth house ending in the sign of Gemini.

Astrological characteristics of the houses briefly described below are intended to give readers a flavor of significance of each of the twelve houses. For readers who want to further pursue their interest, a list of reference material is included in the Bibliography. Again, as I emphasized earlier while presenting the astrological significance of the planets and discussing the individual characteristics of the zodiac signs, **keep in mind that unique characteristics and behavior of an individual, as well as the experiences the individual goes through in his life, are best explained by analyzing the cumulative effect of varying degrees of planetary influence due to their mutual orientation, inter-aspects, the zodiac signs they belong to, and the houses they occupy.** Therefore, the predictions of an individual's character and behavior traits solely based on the characteristics of the person's rising sign could become an embarrassment which an astrologer must avoid.

First

Personality, physical appearance, physical habits, health, vitality, vigor, natural disposition, character, behavior, temperament, life style, determination, courage.

Head, upper part of the face, hair.

Honor, success, dignity, prosperity, fame, happiness.

Beginning, first, rising, birth.

Second

Speech, eating and drinking habits.

Right eye, teeth, tongue, nose, cheeks, chin, vocal cord.

Material wealth, finance, family (parents, brothers, and sisters) matters and heritage, trade, applied knowledge, money.

Conservatism, faith in traditions.

Third

Surroundings, neighbors, short travel, correspondence, communications (letters, telephone, telegrams, internet, etc.), transition, change of residence, transportation.

Ears (especially right ear), throat, shoulder blade, collar bone, arms.

Courage, thoughts, mental strength, will power, restlessness.

Editors, newspaper reporters, journalists.

Libraries, bookstores, battle grounds.

Signature, bargains, rumors.

Fourth

House, home, residence, domestic environment, farm, farmland, cows, milk, orchards, real estate, gardens, buildings, mansions, ancient dwellings, treasures, homeland, automobiles.

Mother, later part of life.

Chest, heart, breasts.

Knowledge, higher education, art.

Secrets, endings, conclusions.

Fifth

Education, learning, wisdom, intelligence, artistic talents, recreation, sports, games, entertainment, music, opera, movies, drama, dance, banquets, romance, relationship, love affairs, physical pleasures, social life, speculations, gambling, betting.

Children, love, marriage, pregnancy.

Hands (especially the right arm and palm).

Envoys, ambassadors.

Sixth

Diseases, sickness, enemy, dangers, debts, sins, wicked act, fear, humiliation, worries, annoyance, jealousy, obstructions, obstacles, theft.

Eating habits, magical spell, superstition.

Job, occupation, work place, employees, assistants, maternal uncles, pets, cattle, sanitation.

Stomach, intestines, right leg.

Seventh

Marriage, married life, wedding, divorce, desire, passion, love, spouse, boss, business partners, joint business, contracts, agreements, competition, rivalry, public adversaries, social life, fines, legal bondage, break of journey, change of residence.

Kidneys, sex organs.

Eighth

Death, longevity, mental pressure and pain, defeat, insult, sorrow, scandal, obstacles, impurity, miseries, misfortune, delay, disappointment, blame, dangers, accidents.

Inheritance, legacies, wills, bonus, insurance.

Legs, bones.

Mysteries.

In-laws, surgeons, medical officers, health inspectors, butchers, slaughter houses, funeral homes, cemeteries.

Flood, fire, famine, earthquakes, epidemics, natural calamities, suicide, violence.

Ninth

Religion, philosophy, wisdom, spiritual strength, worship, prayers, auspicious, fortune, luck, nobility, sacrifices, charity, intuition, faith, divine, morality.

Temples, churches, mosques, synagogues, universities, pilgrimage to holy places, long journeys, long distance communications, moral studies.

Higher knowledge and thoughts, spiritual leaders, philosophers, social reformers, association with inspiring people.

Left hand.

Judges, law, legal arbitration, father.

Import and export of a nation, national trade and commerce.

Tenth

Profession, business, job, career, livelihood, work, occupation, career advancement, business success, appointment, political career, honor, dignity, public esteem, public life, name, fame, power, authority, prestige, popularity, social responsibility, social status, reputation.

Trustees, ambassadors, entrepreneurs, employers, bankers, stockbrokers, superiors, government personnel, father.

Eleventh

Money, profit, financial gains, acquisition, wealth, success, friends, associates, advisors, supporters, well wishers, elder brothers and sisters, desire, passion, pleasure, prosperity, progress, wealth accumulation, wishes, luck, good news.

Left ear.

Parliaments or house of congress, municipalities, town halls, city halls, legislative bodies, local government, government policies and planning, international friendships.

Associations, societies, institutions.

Twelfth

Disappearance, bondage, prison, loss, negation, sin, poverty, misery, decline, sorrow, fear, inferiority complex, impediment, anxiety, misgiving, obstacle, misfortune, persecution, restraint, limitation, waste, extravagance, drudgery, expenses, loan repayment, deception, segregation, suspicion, social barriers, extradition, deportation.

Donation, charity, salvation, divine worship, renunciation of material things.

Intrigue, mystery, secret, solitude, silent sufferings, self-undoing, self-sacrifice, unselfish deeds, seclusion, exile, hospital confinement.

Mental pain and worries, outcasts, unwanted travel, visits to far away places, life in a foreign place, change in surroundings, jails, asylums, sanitariums.

Secret plots, secret enemies, covert operations, conspiracy, frauds, murders, suicide, assassinations, spying, detective work, underground movements.

Left eye.

5. Horoscope Casting

The casting of a horoscope is the first step for an astrological prediction. For a successful astrologer, the degree of confidence in his predictions directly depends on the accuracy of the horoscope he casts. Of course, the method of interpretation is of surmount importance, but even the greatest astrologer can fail in his predictions if the horoscope is not cast with a reasonable accuracy.

In the last chapter, it was mentioned that the basic requirement for casting a horoscope (or a birth chart) of a person is his (or her) birth information, the birth date, place, and the time. In addition, ephemeris and the tables of houses are required. An illustration of how to manually cast a horoscope is provided here. In this illustration, the Raphael's tables of houses and the "World Ephemeris for the 20th Century, 1900-2000 at Noon" by Para Research are used. You may bypass the entire step of the horoscope casting manually, and instead, use a software package. However, the software package must be reliable and should provide reasonably accurate planetary positions and the house cusps for casting the horoscope. Regardless of your choice, the following example details the principle behind the horoscope casting.

For the purpose of illustrating the process of casting a horoscope, an example of the late President Nixon is chosen. Mr. Nixon was born on Thursday, January 9, 1913 at 9:35 p. m. (Pacific Standard Time) in Yorba Linda, California.

The horoscope casting procedure consists of the following steps:

1. Computation of the planetary positions:

First find out the GMT (Greenwich Mean Time) corresponding to the birth time. Since the GMT is exactly 8 hours ahead of the Pacific Standard Time, the corresponding GMT = 5:35 a.m. on January 10, 1913.

Referring to the ephemeris by Para Research, the planetary positions (tropical zodiac longitudes) for noon GMT for January 9 and 10, 1913 are listed in Table 1. The planetary positions for 5:35 a .m. of January 10, 1913 GMT are calculated by linear interpolation, and listed in the last column of the table. An example calculation for Sun is as follows:

Longitude for 5:35 a.m. of January 1913 GMT = (19°-40'-28") - (6:25/24) x (1°-1'-10") = 19°-24'-7"

Note that the planets Saturn, Uranus, and Pluto are retrograde. Also, not listed in the table, the position of Ketu (the descending node of the Moon) being exactly 180 degrees apart from Rahu (the ascending node of the Moon) is 7 degrees and 13 minutes of Libra.

Table 1

Planets	Longitudes for noon January 9, 1913	Longitudes for noon January 10, 1913	Longitudes for 5:35 a.m. January 10, 1913
Sun	18°-39'-18" Capricorn	19°40'-28" Capricorn	**19°24'-7" Capricorn**
Moon	11°-25' Aquarius	23°-17' Aquarius	**20°-07' Aquarius**
Mercury	29°-0' Sagittarius	0°-23' Capricorn	**0°-1' Capricorn**
Venus	2°-38' Pisces	3°-48' Pisces	**3°-29' Pisces**
Mars	29°-12' Sagittarius	29°-57' Sagittarius	**29°-45' Sagittarius**
Jupiter	1°-31' Capricorn	1°-44' Capricorn	**1°-41' Capricorn**
Saturn (R)	27°-31' Taurus	27°-29' Taurus	**27°-30' Taurus**
Uranus	2°-39' Aquarius	2°-42' Aquarius	**2°-41' Aquarius**
Neptune (R)	24°-47' Cancer	24°-46' Cancer	**24°-46' Cancer**
Pluto (R)	28°-40' Gemini	28°-39' Gemini	**28°-39' Gemini**
Rahu	7°-17' Aries	7°-14' Aries	**7°-15' Aries**

2. Computation of the Local Side Real Time

In astronomical calculations, the numerical measure of the time is defined by the diurnal motion of the equinox (or the Vernal Equinox) or by the diurnal motion of the "fixed" stars. In other words, the time it takes for the earth to complete one revolution around its axis, as measured by observing a fixed star or the Vernal Equinox (first point of Aries) is a side real day. It is about 4 minutes short of 24 hours (23 hr. 56 min. 4.09054 sec.) Due to the Earth's motion in its orbit around the Sun, the latter appears to move away nearly by one degree everyday. As a result the Earth has to rotate daily through an extra degree to see the Sun crossing the same meridian in the sky.

The computation of the local side real time at the time of Mr. Nixon's birth is shown as follows:

The longitude and latitude for Yorba Linda are 117°-48' W and 33°-54' N; and the meridian corresponding to the Pacific Standard Time is 120° W.

a. Local time for Yorba Linda = 9 hr. 35 min. + (120 - 117.8) x 4 min. = 9hr. 43.8 min. p.m.

b. Side real time correction for longitude = (117°- 48')/360 x (3 min. 56 sec.) = 1 min. 17 sec.

c. Side real time correction from local mean time to side real interval = (9 hr. 43.8')/24 x (3 min 56 sec.) = 1 min 36 sec.

d. From the ephemeris by Para Search, side real time at Greenwich for noon of Jan 9, 1913 = 19 hr. 13 min. 40 sec.

e. Adding a, b, c, and d, the local side real time at the time of Mr. Nixon's birth is 9 hr. 43.8 min. + 1 min. 17 sec. + 1 min. 36 sec. + 19 hr. 13 min. 40 sec. = 29 hr. 0 min. 21 sec. = 5 hr. 0 min. 21 sec.

3. Computation of the Cusp of the Houses:

Referring to the Raphael's Tables of Houses, for the northern latitude of 33°-54' N, which falls right in the middle of 33°-20' N and 34°-30' N, the cusps of the houses are listed in Table 2 for the side real times 4 hr. 59 min. 10 sec. and 5 hr. 3 min. 29 sec. for 33°-20' N latitude. In the last column of this table the cusp positions for 5 hr. 0 min. 21 sec. side real time are shown after calculating them by linear interpolation.

Table 2

House #	cusp for 33°-20'N and 4 hr. 59 min. 10 sec. side real time	cusp for 33°-20'N and 5 hr. 3 min. 29 sec. side real time	cusp for 33°-20'N and 5 hr. 0 min. 21 sec.
Ascend	17° - 7' Virgo	18°-2' Virgo	17°-22' Virgo
II	13° Libra	14° Libra	13°-17' Libra
III	14° Scorpio	15° Scorpio	14°-17' Scorpio
X	16° Gemini	17° Gemini	16°-17'Gemini
XI	18° Cancer	19° Cancer	18°-17' Cancer
XII	19° Leo	20° Leo	19°-17' Leo

Similarly, in Table 3 the cusps are listed for the side real times 4 hr. 59 min. 10 sec. and 5 hr. 3 min. 29 sec. for 34°-30' N latitude; and in the last column of this table, the cusp positions are calculated for 5 hr. 0 min. 21 sec. side real time by linear interpolation. Finally, in Table 4, the cusp for 33°-54' N latitude and 5 hr. 0 min. 21 sec. side real time is computed by linearly interpolating the results of the last columns of Table 2 and Table 3.

Table 3

House #	cusp for 34°-30'N and 4 hr. 59 min. 10 sec. side real time	cusp for 34°-30'N and 5 hr. 3 min. 29 sec. side real time	cusp for 34°-30'N and 5 hr. 0 min. 21 sec.
Ascend	17° - 14' Virgo	18°-9' Virgo	17°-14' Virgo
II	13° Libra	14° Libra	13°-17' Libra
III	13° Scorpio	14° Scorpio	13°-17' Scorpio
X	16° Gemini	17° Gemini	16°-17'Gemini
XI	19° Cancer	20° Cancer	19°-17' Cancer
XII	19° Leo	20° Leo	19°-17' Leo

Table 4

House #	cusp for 33°-20'N and 5 hr. 0 min. 21 sec. side real time	cusp for 34°-30'N and 5 hr. 0 min. 21 sec. side real time	cusp for 33°-54'N and 5 hr. 0 min. 21 sec.
Ascend	17°-22' Virgo	17°-14' Virgo	**17°-18' Virgo**
II	13°-17' Libra	13°-17' Libra	**13°-17' Libra**
III	14°-17' Scorpio	13°-17' Scorpio	**13°-47' Scorpio**
X	16°-17' Gemini	16°-17' Gemini	**16°-17'Gemini**
XI	18°-17' Cancer	19°-17' Cancer	**18°-47' Cancer**
XII	19°-17' Leo	19° - 17' Leo	**19°-17' Leo**

The cusp of the remaining houses, which are opposite to the houses listed in Table 4, are computed by adding or subtracting exactly 180° to the above listed house cusps. With these results along with the planetary positions listed in Table 1, the moving zodiac system based (Western type) horoscope of Mr. Nixon is shown in Figure 5.1.

For the Eastern Type A horoscope, which is fixed zodiac system based, a correction factor is applied to the moving zodiac positions for both the planets and house cusps according to the following relation:

$$\text{Correction Factor} = 22.3666° - T \times (50.2564 + 0.0222 \times T) / 36$$
$$\text{where } T = (\text{the birth year} - 1900)/100$$

For the birth year 1913, the T equals 0.13, and the correction factor turns out to be 22° - 33'. The correction factor must be subtracted from the moving zodiac system based planetary positions and house cusps to obtain the corresponding information for the fixed zodiac system based horoscope.

It is important to note that except for the ascendant, the Raphael's tables of houses list the house cusps to the nearest degree. Since the computations of the house cusps are done based on linear interpolation for both the side real time and latitude for the birth place and time, the results obtained are accurate within a degree. If a planet falls very near the house cusp, then it is important to have the cusp position calculated as accurately as possible.

The rigorous house cusp calculations based on the equations of planetary motions are listed in Table 5, and the fixed zodiac system based Mr. Nixon's horoscope is shown in Figure 5.2. Note the planetary positions shown in the horoscope are rounded off to the nearest quarter of a degree and the retrograde planets are indicated with the downward arrow.

Table 5: Planetary Positions and House Cusps with Respect to the Fixed Zodiac

House	Cusp Position	Cusp Position based on **rigorous** calc.	Planet	Position
Ascendant	24° - 45' Leo	24° - 52' Leo	Sun	26° - 51' Sagittarius
II	20° - 44' Virgo	21° - 11' Virgo	Moon	27° - 34' Capricorn
III	21° - 14' Libra	21° - 17' Libra	Mercury	7° - 28' Sagittarius
IV	23° - 44' Scorpio	23° - 43' Scorpio	Venus	10° - 56' Aquarius
V	26° - 14' Sagittarius	26° - 15' Sagittarius	Mars	7° - 12' Sagittarius
VI	26° - 44' Capricorn	27° - 00' Capricorn	Jupiter	9° - 8' Sagittarius
VII	24° - 45' Aquarius	24° - 52' Aquarius	Saturn(R)	4° - 57' Taurus
VIII	20° - 44' Pisces	21° - 11' Pisces	Uranus	10° - 8' Capricorn
IX	21° - 14' Aries	21° - 17' Aries	Neptune(R)	2° - 13' Cancer
X	23° - 44' Taurus	23° - 43' Taurus	Pluto(R)	6° - 6' Gemini
XI	27° - 14' Gemini	26° - 15' Gemini	Rahu	14° - 42' Pisces
XII	26° - 44' Cancer	27° - 00' Cancer	Ketu	14° - 42' Virgo

At this point few comments on both of these types of horoscopes are in order.

For any chart the Sun's position immediately reveals the approximate hours through which the person is born. Typically, the Sun in the first house means the birth time is likely to be during 6 to 8 a.m. as the first house indicates the eastern horizon. If it occupies the tenth house, the birth time is probably between the hours of noon through 2 p.m.; similarly, it will be found in the seventh house for an evening (6 to 8 p.m.) born person, and in the

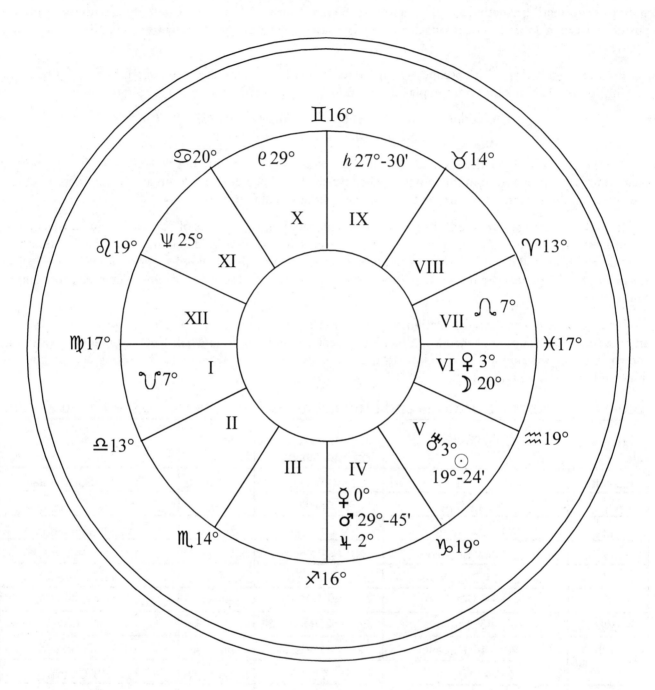

Mr. Nixon's moving zodiac system based (Western type) horoscope.

—Figure 5.1—

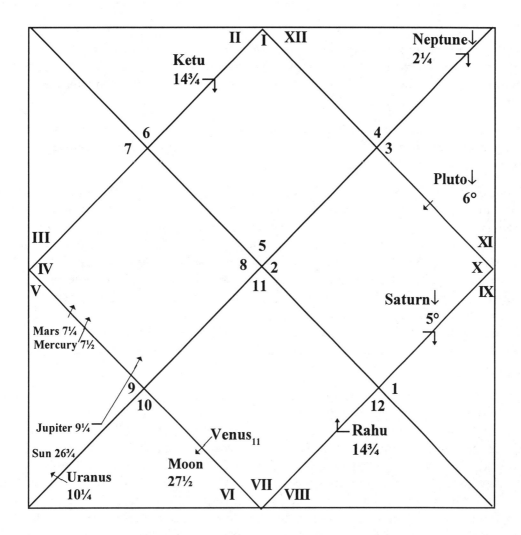

Mr. Nixon's Fixed Zodiac (Eastern Type A) System Based Horoscope

—Figure 5.2—

fourth house for the birth to be around midnight (12 a.m. to 2 a.m.). Of course, this general rule of thumb is likely to be more applicable for the birth places closer to the equator. As the birth place falls on latitudes higher than 20 degrees, the house lengths start becoming more and more disproportional. As a result, the rule seems to fail. However, the deviation is likely to be only by a house in either direction for a given birth time at a higher latitude.

The planet Mercury never gets positioned more than 26 to 27 degrees away from the Sun. If in a horoscope Mercury is positioned in a sextile or square or trine with the Sun, you immediately know the horoscope is inaccurate. Similarly, the maximum distance the planet Venus can have from the Sun's position in the horoscope is approximately 47 degrees.

The exterior planets, when retrograde in motion, are very likely to be positioned in the horoscope more than 90 to 120 degrees away from the Sun. The farther away an exterior planet is, the longer it stays retrograde as its motion becomes retrograde sooner.

It is evident from both types of horoscope formats, as depicted in Figures 5.1 and 5.2, that regardless of the zodiac system employed, the planets occupy the same respective houses. In the moving zodiac system based (Western type) horoscope, the house cusp positions are clearly marked along the circumference. On the other hand, for the fixed zodiac Eastern Type A horoscope (Figure 5.2), the zodiac signs are successively indicated in the respective houses based on the ascendant cusp sign. Planets are shown to be placed in their respective zodiac signs. But they are pointed to their respective houses by an arrow to show the house they belong to. Thus, for example, the planet Saturn being in Taurus (5° Taurus), is shown to be placed in the tenth house; but the tenth cusp being 23° - 44' of Taurus, the Saturn's ninth house residence is indicated by the arrow pointing towards ninth house. Similarly, the planet Venus is in sixth house and in Aquarius sign. Usually, the cusp degrees are not shown in the eastern charts. With a table of house cusp list, the house to which a planet belongs, wherever appropriate, is shown by an arrow pointing to the house.

One of the reasons I prefer the Eastern Type A format of the horoscope over the Western is the way it directly allows me to visualize the person. Just looking at the horoscope I can start sketching the person with the first house describing his face and personality, with the second and twelfth houses his eyes, with the third and eleventh his ears, with the fourth and tenth his chest, heart and stomach, with the fifth and ninth his arms and hands, with the sixth and eighth his thighs and legs, and finally with the seventh house his kidneys and sexual organ. Of course, there are other things which I could also include based on the characteristics of the houses described in the previous chapter. This helps me in verifying the accuracy of the person's birth time. Usually the given birth time is not very precise due to either its unavailability, vague recollection, or guess work. If the person's appearance I just described doesn't quite match, I don't continue his (or her) horoscope analysis. It saves me a lot of my horoscope interpretation and prediction time. And most importantly, when my predicted description of the person matches with his (or her) appearance, it gives me a lot better degree of confidence in helping the person with his (or her) specific needs and questions.

The importance of an accurate birth time will only gain public acceptance if people's perception of astrology becomes positive. That can only happen when the successful application of astrology for individual charts begins to materialize. When and if that happens, the hospitals would be forced to give serious consideration in keeping the record of birth time accurate to the nearest minute for every baby they deliver. And that situation would tremendously enhance the further development in astrology as astrologers would no longer have to deal with laborious trial and error method and guesswork in estimating the accurate birth time for prediction purposes.

6. House-Planet Connection

In this chapter, the influence of a planet on an individual by occupying a certain house in his natal chart is described for all planets and their possible house occupancy scenarios. Again, this information is intended to be general source material, and the specific inference and subsequent astrological interpretation will depend on several other factors as will be illustrated later in the horoscope analysis/interpretation chapter. Unless it is exclusively stated, the information provided here is only applicable if the house is occupied by the planet under consideration alone and other planets don't influence the house either by angular aspect or by the particular configuration. Usually it is a rare case when the result indicated by the presence of a planet in a house doesn't get modified due to other planetary effects on that house. In what follows, unless it is explicitly stated, the reference to the masculine gender also includes the feminine gender; for example, the reference to "he" and "him," also implicitly include "she" and "her."

Sun

First House: Sun in the first house makes one proud, generous, confident, and strong. The person usually has a big forehead and a round face. Social prestige and respect come naturally to this person.

Second House: The general characteristics of a person with the Sun in this house are generosity, big spender, egoist. In the presence of the malicious planets like Mars or Uranus in the second house, the person could experience frequent financial crisis; he may have problems with his eyes, teeth, or throat. With Rahu or Saturn in the second house, the person could lose his entire fortune; but with auspicious planet Jupiter in the second house, financially, he probably will do very well.

Third House: This is one of the positive houses for Sun to occupy. The person is very likely to have the following qualities: independent, self-confident, self-made, self-starter, determined, achiever, intelligent, just, analytical, honest, straightforward, realistic.

Fourth House: Usually the fourth house in not desirable for Sun to fall in. With an evil planet, his relationship with his mother is likely to remain strained if not worse. Also, the person tends to become accident prone, may have a weak heart. Probably unhappy at home.

Fifth House: The person probably has a tendency to act up. With an auspicious planet, the person is likely to finish higher education; he is likely to be fond of his children. With an evil planet, however, the relationship with children can be very strenuous. With Mercury in the fifth house expect interest in research.

Sixth House: Good for job as the Sun in the sixth house makes the person active, efficient. Likely to get frequent promotions and powerful positions at work. If the Sun is with Mars, the health problems (orthoscopic surgeries, cardiac arrests, etc.) are likely to occur more often. Since the planets in the twelfth house directly affect the sixth house planets, the malicious twelfth house resident planets are more likely to bring the person misfortune, tragedies, and downfalls.

Seventh House: The seventh house Sun could mean the person's spouse is a strong and determined person.

Eighth House: The person is less likely to have financial stability or it comes late in life. The person is likely to suffer a series of setbacks in life.

Ninth House: Well behaved, well mannered person. He is a hardworking ambitious person. He gets well deserved social prestige. In general, he is likely to have his desires fulfilled.

Tenth House: This is probably the ideal house to have the Sun in if the person is looking for social and political power and fame. People working for government with prestigious positions are very likely to have the Sun positioned in the tenth house in their horoscopes.

Eleventh House: Eleventh house Sun keeps money flowing in. The person's financial prosperity grows phenomenally, and he is likely to become a powerful social figure.

Twelfth House: The Sun in this house creates unfavorable situations in a person's life. The common characteristics are disappointments, insult, social problems. With the Sun and Saturn conjunction in this house, even the innocent person is likely to get arrested and sent to prison.

Moon

First House: Unless it is affected by an unfavorable planet, Moon in this house virtually guarantees good health all throughout life. The person has a charming personality; he is loving, compassionate, sensitive, gentle. The person is lively, well mannered, smart, sharp, and perhaps moody.

Second House: With Moon alone in the second house, the person is talkative, has a melodious voice, and beautiful eyes. Unless the second house is affected by an unfavorable planet, financially the person is bound to do well. With Venus in the second house he may have a career in music or singing.

Third House: Moon in the third house means the person is very fond of his kin and vice versa. He is loving, caring, emotional, shy, and moody. He may have various interests and hobbies. His travel particularly includes short journeys.

Fourth House: In the absence of effects due to unfavorable planets, Moon makes the person wealthy, happy, and gives good family life. He probably remains very attached to his mother. Generally the later part of his life is very satisfying and filled with joy.

Fifth House: Moon in the fifth house makes the person artistic, happy, and intelligent. He has loving children. He may develop gambling tendencies.

Sixth House: In this house Moon feels suffocated. Unless it receives beneficial influence from Jupiter, Venus, or Neptune the person is likely to be mentally very weak, unsteady, with no self-esteem. He is likely to blame others or situations that he is unable to handle. With the planet like Saturn or Mars in the sixth house, unless the ascendant is strong with the presence of a beneficial planet, he is likely to stay unhealthy with a long term illness or a frequent short term health problem.

Seventh House: With Moon alone in the seventh house, the person is likely to have a spouse with completely complementary characteristics; as a result, his marriage is likely to be happy, and probably is likely to last until death do they part. Expect the opposite when the Moon is in conjunction with Mars in the seventh without any positive influence from an auspicious planet. Seventh house Moon indicates long journeys!

Eighth House: In general, this Moon is not positive. With Jupiter and/or Venus in the eighth; however, the person may strike big money either through inheritance or some other way. With unfavorable planets like Uranus, Mars, or Saturn he is likely to suffer through a series of disappointments and failures during the periods when the effects of the unfavorable planets become active.

Ninth House: This is probably the most suitable house for Moon to be in. With auspicious planets like Jupiter or Neptune in the fifth house, the person is likely to excel in the field of education. He is religious and probably takes an active role in the religious activities helping the needy. He may acquire fame and prestige. He is likely to visit places overseas. Financially, he is fortunate.

Tenth House: Moon alone in the tenth house means a constant change in job or profession or sometimes in career. But with other planets in the tenth, Moon can be a real blessing. It bestows the person with social prestige.

Eleventh House: The eleventh house Moon makes one rich and provides a big friend circle, mostly females. The person is very fond of his daughters. In general, he is likely to enjoy all sorts of material pleasures in his life.

Twelfth House: From a material world standpoint this is not a good house for Moon. The person is likely to be all the time worrying, unsure, and mentally confused. He may have to face sudden bankruptcy in his life. With Rahu or Saturn misfortune will follow him, and his eyesight could get seriously strained and he may become blind as a result.

Mercury

First House: Mercury in the first house alone makes one very talkative, social, witty, and street smart. The person usually appears to be younger than his age. An ever smiling face makes him a successful salesperson. Usually he shows a keen sense of presence of mind. He is always curious about things around him, has a good analytical mind, and a good expressive power. Other characteristics are: studious, sharp, political, diplomatic, clever, cunning. With proper support from Mars (with a trine or sextile angle), he could do well in the field of engineering. With Uranus he may achieve a high level of success in scientific research. Venus will enhance his conversational skills.

Second House: With Mercury alone in the second house, the person is likely to be very talkative, and probably a good debater. He has a potential for becoming a successful person in the field of finance, such as a broker, an equity manager, a banker, a merger and acquisition lawyer, or a dealer. He may have an uncanny ability to express his imagination, and thus, he could become a successful writer. With Venus in the second house he may pursue a career in singing. He is typically very creative, pragmatic, down to earth, and loves to read.

Third House: The general characteristics of Mercury in the third house are extreme curiosity, fast learner, excellent analytical and sharp mind. Such a person has a good chance of becoming a successful detective or a mystery solver. His dominant reading and writing skills, and a powerful research mind, may make him a mystery writer. He has a strong affinity to his younger kin. He enjoys short travel. He may be good in accounting with his sharp arithmetic skills, or he could excel as a newspaper publisher, editor, or like. With Venus in the third house he could pursue a career in music, with Neptune in the third house he could develop interest in astrology or occult, while with Uranus he could become a moody scientist. With the third house cusp falling in a dual sign (Gemini, Virgo, Sagittarius, and Pisces) he may have various interests and hobbies.

Fourth House: In the absence of effects due to unfavorable planets, Mercury makes the person loving, talkative and happy. He probably has a lot of good friends and relations. He often tends to get homesick and probably remains very attached to his mother.

Fifth House: Mercury in the fifth house propels the person towards higher educational pursuits. With good support from Mars or Uranus he could become a successful scientist, a science or an engineering professor. With Neptune in the fifth house, Mercury tends to expand his interest in the psychic and mysterious areas.

Sixth House: In this house Mercury doesn't get motivated. Unless it receives beneficial influence from Jupiter, the person is likely to pick fights. The circumstances will probably encourage him to lie. He may not be perceived as trustworthy. He is likely to end up spending his time quarreling with his enemies.

Seventh House: With Mercury alone in the seventh house, the person is likely to have a happy situation with his spouse. But with Mars or Uranus in the seventh, Mercury becomes helpless, bringing out the worst in his marriage.

Eighth House: In general, this Mercury is not positive. With unfavorable planets like Uranus, Mars, or Saturn in this house with Mercury, the person is likely to suffer through a series of financial setbacks and perhaps mental disorder.

Ninth House: Mercury in the ninth house gives wisdom, knowledge, fame, luck, manners, and makes one a respected person in society. He is likely to pursue a career as a writer or a talk show host with a great deal of success. Usually he is shrewd, curious, and perhaps good at detective work. He enjoys visiting places and leisure readings. With auspicious planets like Jupiter or Neptune in the ninth house he is likely to get involved in religious activities.

Tenth House: Mercury alone in the tenth house means an entrepreneur, a true business person, or an excellent salesman. Due to his humorous nature he may become a successful comedian or a witty talk show host. In general, he is creative, smart, and an excellent planner. He is a good judge of people.

Eleventh House: The eleventh house Mercury means the person has a big friend circle that includes mostly younger ones. He is very fond of his friends. He is very social, a true extrovert. He is talkative, and does well in his business.

Twelfth House: Twelfth house Mercury alone or with Mars or Uranus, is likely to make one a liar and a crook. He is likely to get involved in matters that will get him in trouble. However, with Jupiter or Saturn in the twelfth house he may travel to far away places and would develop interest in mysterious things.

Venus

First House: Venus in the first house makes the person attractive, charming, and sensuous. He probably has very expressive eyes. He tends to be a fashion freak, social, and very amiable. His major goal in life is the pursuit of material pleasure and to enjoy life. He has a natural inclination towards art, dance, and music. He is very loving and caring, and most likely to have a good marriage.

Second House: Unless there is a malicious planet in the second or eighth house, the person is gifted with the most beautiful and lively eyes, and a very sweet voice. He probably comes from a rich family with a good upbringing and happy childhood. He is usually wealthy, lucky, and has a true taste for good food. Females with second house Venus are likely to be bestowed with real jewelry, gold, diamonds, gems, pearls, and stones.

Third House: A person with a true love for art, music, travel, and nature usually has Venus in the third house in his horoscope. Venus as the only planet in the third house means he is very likely to have a younger sister, and he cares for her a lot. He has a natural tendency to be appreciative, to help and care for others. He is likely to have beautiful handwriting. Poets and writers usually have Venus placed in the third house of their horoscopes.

Fourth House: If alone in the fourth house, Venus makes the person very happy and loving. His Natural disposition is towards loving and caring for others. He has a good domestic life. He is good at heart. Generally he enjoys his life, owns real estate, and cares for his mother.

Fifth House: This is one of the most desirable houses for Venus. Venus in this house is excellent for pursuing any artistic hobby. The person usually has a natural craving for art. Typically, he is a perfect gentleman as evident through his good manners and politeness. A perfect extrovert too! He is social, a naturalist, sensuous, romantic, and very loving. He enjoys material pleasures in life. He is very intimate with his children.

Sixth House: Not a happy situation to have Venus in the sixth house! Typically qualities of such a person are notorious, weird, lazy, anti-social, unhappy, some flaw in character, prodigal. A constant occurrence of natural hindrances keep his artistic abilities from being developed.

Seventh House: Sensuous, good sex life, and perhaps a good married life. The person gets married early. He is likely to have fortunate events occur right after his wedding. Usually his spouse dominates his life and brings a lot of luck in his life.

Eighth House: Venus alone in the eighth house keeps the person out of financial troubles. With Jupiter or Moon in the eighth he may experience unexpected financial windfalls in his life, such as lottery, inheritance of wealth and real estate. His relationship with his in-laws is usually very warm.

Ninth House: Venus in this house brings fame, fortune, and showers the person with all sorts of material happiness. This Venus makes one very generous, religious, kind, open and broad minded, and very caring. He pursues art, loves reading, enjoys travel, and has good times with his children.

Tenth House: Venus in the tenth house creates very easy situations for job and career. Instead of looking for an opportunity, opportunities chase the person. Consequently, he gets fame, popularity, good social prestige, and of course, a lot of money. He is very amiable and doesn't really have to deal with obstacles in his professional life.

Eleventh House: This Venus provides excellent financial stability through a good job and a lot of helpful friends. He has a very good temperament and manners. He is loving, caring, likable, and generous. He cares for his children a lot. He may be very close to his older sister or brother, and they are fond of each other.

Twelfth House: As far as (sexual) relationships go the twelfth house Venus is eccentric. He is likely to have extra marital affairs. He is secretive, unethical, and has some flaw in his character. He is likely to be notorious. His married life usually remains an unhappy one.

Mars

First House: Mars in the first house makes one very energetic and strong. The person may be tall, with a bit of reddish eyes. He is perceived as an impatient, impulsive, aggressive, and an ambitious person. He is confident, determined, insistent, hardworking, very independent, and a true self-starter. Anger and perhaps revenge might be his biggest weaknesses. But he never lets up. He loves power, loves to command others, and, therefore, it's no wonder he has a natural inclination towards politics or the corporate world where he can exercise his authority and power. He may have a birthmark on his face. If Mars is associated with either Uranus or one of the lunar nodes (Rahu or Ketu), he tends to be accident prone and frequently causes injuries to himself.

Second House: Mars in the second house is generally a difficult situation. The person is very industrious and possessive. He is bold, but due to his impatient and impulsive nature he is a poor money manager. He may get in trouble due to his over generous characteristics. He may incur some problems with his eyes. He is argumentative. In association with Mercury in this house he has a potential for successfully pursuing a career as a debater or a critic. He is likely to be perceived as a bashful, impolite rascal. He loves meat, spicy, and greasy food. If inflicted with Uranus, expect at least a few financial turmoils in his life.

Third House: The third house is suitable for enhancing the positive qualities of Mars. The person is adventures, courageous, a risk taker, and usually successful in his ventures. He is a strong soldier; and his general characteristics include: fearlessness, adamant, assertiveness, impulsiveness, and he loves difficult challenges. His handwriting probably shows sharp angles and narrow hooks.

Fourth House: Mars alone in the fourth house without any positive support from other planets either through association, angle, or aspect creates turbulent atmosphere in the person's home (family) life. The person tends to be accident prone (especially if the Mars is with Uranus in this house). Usually he experiences difficulties in the latter part of his life. His relationship with his mother is likely to be strenuous. His mother may have a serious and chronic illness.

Fifth House: The person may not get along with his own children. For females, it's very likely to have a miscarriage or a similar problem at the time of delivery. He may develop gambling tendencies and perhaps lose money.

Sixth House: Due to the sixth house Mars, the person may have frequent acute fevers, chicken pox, measles, mumps, inflammatory complaints, burns, hemorrhage, bleeding. He is likely to have at least a few surgical operations in his life. This Mars, however, is excellent for his profession. He would, most of the time, be victorious over his enemies. His enemies would usually be scared of him.

Seventh House: Seventh house Mars means the person is very likely to have a spouse who is aggressive, impatient, and impulsive. He may have a problem of getting along with his spouse, and they may separate as a result. Also, he may experience problems in getting along with his business partners or with his superiors in his profession.

Eighth House: Unless it is influenced by a beneficial planet, the Mars in the eighth house alone brings financial misfortunes to the person.

Ninth House: Mars in the ninth house is usually responsible for a person's success, fame, and heroic deeds. The person is very independent and self-made. He is likely to be a doctor or an engineer. He loves sports and is likely to be a natural athlete.

Tenth House: The tenth house Mars makes one very ambitious, energetic, and an excellent fighter. He is an opportunist and power hungry. He is exceptionally adventurous, very dynamic, and fast acting. He is a winner! He loves challenges, and loves beating his opponents against all odds. He is likely to make frequent professional changes to rise to the top.

Eleventh House: Mars in the eleventh house makes one possessive, hard working, and successful! The person is likely to be perceived as bashful, and may have very few friends. He is likely to have trouble getting along with his own children.

Twelfth House: From the seventh house standpoint, the twelfth house Mars is not a happy situation. The person is likely to be misunderstood. He has a natural inclination to be drawn into a quarrel or fight. He may experience problems with his eyes. A bankruptcy and going to a prison are real possibilities in his life.

Jupiter

First House: Typical characteristics of a person with Jupiter in the first house of his horoscope are happy, optimist, matured, quiet, law abiding, social, sportsman, and generous. He may look a bit chubby, and is likely to have prominent two middle teeth. He has an analytical mind; he is self-confident and a good judge of character. He is lucky, and popularity and fame follow him. He may be a linguist.

Second House: The second house Jupiter generally indicates the person was born in a large and a well to do family. Continuous flux of incoming money virtually assures a sound financial condition in his life. He may have a tendency to overeat.

Third House: The person is loving and caring. He is studious, loves reading, and usually receives a good education.

Fourth House: General tendency for this Jupiter is to create and maintain happy surroundings against all odds. He generally has a good family life. He is likely to be closely attached to his mother.

Fifth House: This is a good house to have Jupiter in. With an analytical and research mind, the person has little trouble finishing higher education. Being a scholar and linguist, his natural inclination is to pursue a career in the field of education. Professors, teachers, scientists, psychologists, philosophers, writers, and editors probably have Jupiter in the fifth house of their horoscopes or some connection between the tenth and fifth houses through Jupiter.

Sixth House: Jupiter in the sixth house is not exactly well placed except that it supports tenth house, the house of profession, and provides the person with professional and financial stability. Also, from a financial standpoint, the sixth house Jupiter is positive for his maternal uncle and his family. On the down side, the sixth house Jupiter may cause him frequent indigestion. With Mars in the sixth house with Jupiter, he is likely to have stomach related surgical operation. He may become an anemic.

Seventh House: The seventh house Jupiter is good for marriage and financial stability.

Eighth House: Jupiter in the eighth house is supposed to indicate that the person will have a financial windfall at least a few times in his life. However, in my opinion, that can only happen when the fifth and eleventh houses are unaffected by the malicious planets. In addition, the placing of Venus and Moon in the horoscope must strengthen Jupiter's position.

Ninth House: This is an excellent house for realizing all good things that Jupiter can offer. By definition, the person is lucky! He will earn respect and reputation through his deeds. He is intelligent, craves knowledge, and is likely to achieve a high position in the field of education. He is a self starter. He is very likely to be interested in religion and spiritual matters. He is brilliant. He may become a writer, a philosopher, or a social or political figure.

Tenth House: Tenth house Jupiter means a person's work place is more likely to be in schools, colleges, universities, religious institutes, or educational departments. He may be a teacher, a professor, a preacher, or the like. He has a social prestige; and being famous and likable, he is well respected in the society.

Eleventh House: The person is a true friend, a perfect gentleman, honest, loving, and amiable. He is very social and well respected. He is wealthy. He is probably the one who realizes most of his wishes in his life.

Twelfth House: Twelfth house Jupiter provides a good foundation for spiritual life. The person is least interested in acquiring material things. He is very kind, loving, human, forgiving, and generous. He seeks knowledge to understand life and to be free from life's drudgeries. He is probably a philosopher, a hermit, and lives a very austere life.

Saturn

First House: If a person looks older than his age and rarely has a natural smile on his face, it's very likely that Saturn is positioned in the first house in his horoscope. His typical characteristics are mature, pessimist, patient, dull, lazy, laconic, and introverted. Until he reaches age thirty-six, he probably goes through a series of difficult times. There are often "delays" in his life. He is likely to get married late in his life. In association with the unfavorable planets in the first house, his troubles in his life are intensified and last long.

Second House: The second house Saturn makes one very pragmatic, practical, and conservative when it comes to handling money. He is a hard working, quiet person who won't spend a penny unless he has given a serious thought to the matter. With Jupiter in the second house, he is unlikely to experience any financial trouble in his life. With Venus in the second house, he probably will accumulate a lot of wealth. But with unfavorable planets like Mars or Uranus in the second house, he is likely to face frequent financial crises; also he is likely to develop eye and teeth problems.

Third House: Saturn in the third house makes one a serious thinker. He is normally a calm and peaceful person. He is patient, courageous, and only takes calculated risks. He usually does well in his life. He is an achiever and an ambitious person. He probably doesn't have younger kin, or if he had one he would have difficulty in getting along with his kin.

Fourth House: Fourth house Saturn may cause an early death to the person's mother, or his relationship with his mother will probably always remain strenuous. He is likely to have sad childhood memories.

Fifth House: Saturn in the fifth house means the person is shrewd and very selfish. He is very clever, political, intelligent, diplomatic, and a realist. He is skeptical, suspicious, and perhaps unreliable. He is very patient, and usually successfully pursues his educational ambition. With Mercury, Jupiter, and Uranus in the first or in the ninth house of his horoscope, he can achieve a very high career goal in his life. Also, this Saturn is good for pursuing a career in law.

Sixth House: This is not a favorable house for Saturn to bloom. In general, the person is easily misunderstood, has a natural tendency to create enemies, and has no difficulty in getting himself involved in a fight. As a result, he is always worried and annoyed. In addition, he faces a lot of obstacles and misfortunes in his life. Stability arrives late in life. He is likely to have poor health, long illnesses, arthritis, and perhaps likely to experience a paralysis attack.

Seventh House: The person with Saturn in the seventh house usually gets married late in his life. With Mars or Uranus in the seventh house he is very likely to have problems in his marriage, and probably end up with a divorce or two. With Neptune in the seventh house he is unlikely to get married.

Eighth House: Saturn being the planet of death, the eighth house Saturn is supposed to provide the person with a long life. However, he may have to face a series of obstacles, unnecessary situations, and delays in his life. With a planet like Mars or Uranus in the eighth house he is likely to remain mired in a constant financial and physical struggle in his life.

Ninth House: The ninth house Saturn makes the person an orthodox and an ultra conservative. He is generally intelligent, just, and patient. He is likely to become a lawyer, a religious authority, or a research scientist.

Tenth House: Saturn alone in the tenth house without being influenced by any unfavorable planet usually means the person is going to achieve the highest goal he can set in his life. It might take all his life, but he will be successful and become somebody worth remembering after he is long gone. He is ambitious, egoistic, and very shrewd. He enjoys social prestige. He may not get along with his father.

Eleventh House: This Saturn is good for pursuing a career in law. The person usually has very few friends. He is typically a true introvert. He is always extremely careful with any financial dealing. He is a good planner, a hard worker, and very self-centered.

Twelfth House: The person with the twelfth house Saturn in his horoscope is likely to struggle with adverse situations in his life for a long time. He is not blessed to have enough opportunities in his life. Usually an opportunity comes very late in life. Typical characteristics of this Saturn are unlucky, unfortunate, delays, problems, disappointments, pessimism. In association with unfavorable planets like Mars, Sun, or Uranus in the twelfth house the situation becomes worse. He is likely to frequently suffer from unexpected and sudden financial losses; he is likely to get arrested even if he is innocent, or have a terrible accident. Saturn alone in this house, however, makes the person spiritually strong.

Uranus

First House: Uranus in the first house creates a strange personality. The person acts and behaves in a totally unconventional manner. He is moody, absolutely unpredictable, and appears to be totally disconnected. He seems unsure, whimsical, but very brilliant. He is unorthodox, very independent, self-centered, and self-oriented. He has tremendous stamina and energy, very dynamic and quick in action. He loves to overpower people in a very subtle way. He is fearless, confident, impatient, and perhaps imprudent. He may be bald, mischievous, and exhibits childlike behavior. In association with the Sun, Saturn, or Mars, the dark side of his personality gets intensified. He meets serious accidents, fails miserably in his endeavors, and is likely to have serious burns or get hit by explosives. On the other hand, with Uranus and auspicious planets like Mercury or Jupiter, his research faculties get fully activated; he then solves very difficult and mysterious problems in a very short time. He is shrewd and an excellent planner. First house Uranus usually puts him in a divorce situation at least once in his life.

Second House: The second house Uranus means financial turmoil and instability. The person incurs unexpected and sudden losses and expenditures. He is likely to be perceived as bad mouthed and bashful. With Mercury in the second house, Uranus in the second usually makes him a strong critic.

Third House: A person is likely to be blessed with a tremendous intellectual and thinking power by the third house Uranus. Excellent grasping power accompanied by a sharp analytical mind, extreme curiosity, and a photographic memory are the main characteristics of the third house Uranus. With Mercury or Jupiter in the third house, he is likely to achieve remarkable feats in the areas of scientific research and the like. The person loves mystery solving. He travels to far away places. His handwriting is likely to be weird.

Fourth House: The person with Uranus in the fourth house of his horoscope is likely to be miserable in his life. He has trouble getting along with his family members, and with his mother, in particular. He is very insistent, often tends to lose his temper, and perhaps very accident prone. He doesn't stay at one place for a long time; he changes his jobs frequently.

Fifth House: This house provides proper nourishment for Uranus's intellectual capabilities. Uranus all by itself is probably not that effective in this house, but with Mercury or Jupiter either in the fifth house or in the trine, the Uranus makes the person extraordinarily brilliant. For scientific research, inventions, and discoveries he is most ideally suited. The rapid technological growth is only possible with the planets like Uranus or Pluto acting as a catalyst for Mercury, Jupiter, and Venus. He pursues challenges of unfolding the mysteries of the universe. He has a strong interest in mystical things. He may develop gambling tendencies, and perhaps lose a lot of money in gambling or betting. For women, Uranus alone in the fifth house indicates a miscarriage, or problems at the time of delivery.

Sixth House: This is not a good house for Uranus to reside. The person may be mentally unstable; at times he may experience memory loss. He is likely to run into health related problems, especially the ones that deal with the brain. With Mars in the sixth house he is likely to have a serious illness, bad fire burns, or accidents with electricity. With Rahu or Mercury in the sixth house, he could become possessed. From the profession or job (tenth house) standpoint, Uranus is really helpful to him by encouraging and supporting the tenth house related activities.

Seventh House: The significance of having the Uranus in the seventh house is similar to that of Mars in the seventh; the only difference is with the Uranus the results get dramatically intensified. The spouse is likely to be unorthodox, whimsical, and moody. The marriage is not on sound footing. Constant fights and frustration are likely to exist between the spouses. Also, he is equally unfortunate to have a rough relationship with his superior at work. His competitors are likely to have an edge over him. In court battles, he is likely to be defeated. With a planet like Mars or Saturn in the seventh house, he is likely to experience a series of unhappy relationships and a handful of divorces in his life. With Venus in the seventh house, an extra marital affair is a good probability.

Eighth House:	Uranus alone and particularly near the cusp in the eighth house is bad news. The person is likely to experience financial setbacks, run into serious accidents, get involved with undesired people, and end up in misery.
Ninth House:	Uranus in the ninth house means overseas travel, visiting far away places, and in some cases migrating to a far away country. The person is likely to have a deep interest in nature, astrology, occult, magic, and mystical things. With his brilliant scientific mind he is very capable of pursuing scientific research leading to major discoveries and inventions. His fertile imagination can be positively utilized in applied research to create new products and devices, efficient methods for industrial manufacturing. From a religious standpoint, he is likely to be either neutral or an atheist. He may have his own unorthodox philosophy.
Tenth House:	"Constant change in job or profession" is the key significance of this Uranus. With an auspicious planet either in conjunction or in trine with Uranus, the person moves up the career ladder amazingly fast. He is extremely independent, highly open minded, and always willing to try new things. He works very hard to reach his goal. He is very diplomatic, professional, and shrewd. In association with an unfavorable planet in the tenth house, however, he ends up spending a good part of his life facing the obstacles with very little or no success.
Eleventh House:	This Uranus makes the person's financial situation very unstable. He doesn't quite get along well with his friends. With an auspicious planet in the eleventh house, he is likely to experience a financial windfall.
Twelfth House:	Expect continuous financial problems. Also, the person is likely to experience traumatic situations in his life. Shame in public, social embarrassment and insulting treatment are some of the things he will experience in his life. He is likely to be associated with the wrong people.

Neptune

First House:	Neptune in the first house makes the person extremely sensitive to his surroundings and emotions. His physical appearance is very fragile. He always seems nervous and is likely to be a pessimist. But he tends to become a source of inspiration for others due to his powerful inner strength. He is likely to be dreamy, but he is usually closer to reality than a normal person can be. In the company of unfavorable planets like Mars, Saturn, or Rahu in the first house he is likely to become weak by inflicting himself with a mental disease.
Second House:	The person is likely to get in deep financial trouble since Neptune is the worst planet for handling finance. He may assume undue responsibilities and cause financial problems to others.
Third House:	Neptune in this house makes the person more inclined to spiritual and mystical matters. He has a wonderful gift of imagination, inspiration, and intuition. He is extremely sensitive and compassionate. With Mercury in the third house, his mental faculties become extraordinarily powerful. Neptune enhances the positive qualities of the third house Venus, Mercury, or Moon to an unimaginable level. With unfavorable planets (like Mars, Rahu, or Ketu) in the third house he becomes mentally very weak. Neptune is also responsible for long travel and visits or migration to far away places.
Fourth House:	The fourth house Neptune tends to cause concerns, misunderstanding and anxieties in family matters. In general, Neptune is favorable to this house only when it is in conjunction with either Moon, Jupiter, or Venus.

Fifth House: The fifth house Neptune blesses the person with the gift of intuition, divine power, and extrasensory perception. As a result, he can feel events before they happen. He is very likely to have spiritual experiences in life. He has the potential to become a successful magician and an expert in hypnotism and mystical power. Spiritually he is already advanced. He has a very fertile imagination. With Venus in the fifth house he is likely to make a great deal of progress in the areas of art, music, literature, and writing. Feelings of Neptune are not of the material world but of the spiritual world. This is a very important distinction between Neptune and Venus. Venetian love requires the other person (or body) to participate in the process, but Neptunian love doesn't need the presence of the other person. Neptunian feelings are extreme and real! With Mercury in the fifth house, he may have the sharpest mind and an uncanny ability to solve any mind boggling mystery; while with Moon in the fifth house, he is likely to achieve the extraordinarily awake state, the ultimate of the spiritual world.

Sixth House: Neptune in the sixth house makes a perfectly normal person unnecessarily worry about his health. Usually such people are scared of any disease. Along with Moon in the sixth house, Neptune makes matters worse by making the person mentally extremely weak and unsteady. Also, it could cause the person a neurodisorder and insomnia. He is likely to suffer from betrayal and deceit.

Seventh House: Not a good situation from a marriage standpoint! The person is likely to have a rough and bumpy ride in his married life. Even at the time of his wedding, Neptune puts its mark with some strange happening. Based on the study of several horoscopes, I noticed that Neptune alone in the seventh house in a fire sign doesn't promise marriage. But in a water sign with a favorable influence from either Venus, Jupiter, or Moon, he is likely to have a normal happy marriage.

Eighth House: Neptune in the eighth house may create a situation of a mysterious death or disappearance. In association with an evil planet in the eighth house, out of desperation, the person may try to kill himself. By mistake he may poison himself. Financially he needs to watch out for unexpected and sudden losses.

Ninth House: This is probably the most ideal house to have Neptune in. The auspicious ninth house Neptune elevates the person's spiritual capabilities to a very high level. His dreams are lively and meaningful. His senses are extremely aware, and his intuition power is at its best. He travels around the world, visits many places, and meets a lot of people. With an unfavorable planet in the ninth house he becomes a fake.

Tenth House: The person changes his job very frequently. He moves a lot too! Generally, he is likely to be lazy and a coward. With Venus in the tenth house he should consider pursuing a career as a magician, a psychiatrist, or a psychic. In association with Saturn or Mars in the tenth house, he is likely to lose big in his business, experience a downfall in his profession, or have to deal with social scandals and political setbacks.

Eleventh House: This Neptune causes unnecessary delays in financial matters that mostly result in loss. The person is likely to have too much confidence in his friends who would cheat on him. He tends to surround himself with the wrong people.

Twelfth House: The twelfth house Neptune makes one worrisome, mentally tense, and nervous. The person is very likely to be a pessimist. He is likely to work for or deal with a spy agency or social institution. In conjunction with Mars he is likely to experience unnecessary situations in his life that are totally uncalled for. Physical abuse, being framed for a crime he didn't commit, fine, and prison confinement are a few possibilities. With Saturn in the twelfth house, the situation is likely to stay the same with one exception. If that Saturn receives a favorable support from Jupiter, he is likely to experience remarkable spiritual progress in his life. Also, he is likely to become a philosopher or a humanist.

Pluto

According to many astrologers, the effects of the planet Pluto alone on an individual are considered unimportant. The reason: not enough information has been gathered and analyzed to establish the correlation of Pluto's motion with its influence on individuals. However, based on the available information, the general consensus among astrologers is that Pluto's power is usually tapped by the planets that come in its association or make favorable or unfavorable angles with it. If placed uniquely in a horoscope, Pluto can make a big difference! The influence of Pluto at a collective level, such as on a nation or a continent, has been studied by several astrologers. The results seem to indicate that matters such as wars, big upheavals in a country or at a place, are connected to Pluto's motion and position across the zodiacs.

Based on my limited experience, I would like to share the following to describe the influence of Pluto on an individual.

Pluto is a planet of a tremendous power, and depending on how that power gets channeled, Pluto can become either constructive or destructive for a person. The channeling of its power is generally brought about through planets that are slower moving than Uranus. Usually one in a thousand, or maybe in ten thousand, has a planetary configuration in his horoscope where Pluto's effect is worth considering. I have observed that if the planet Pluto is on the cusp of a house (within a degree or so) and influences a planet through a particular angle, then Pluto is likely to play a very important role in that person's life. Depending upon the house, the house cusp ruler, and the planet(s) it influences, Pluto's energy gets manifested in a unique manner.

Rahu

The influence of Rahu on an individual through a house occupation is, in general, very similar to that of Saturn. For a start, what's been said for Saturn earlier in this chapter can be directly applicable for Rahu. But Rahu's unique influence on an individual must be analyzed through other considerations. For example, Rahu acts as a catalyst by directly providing either positive or negative boost to a planet through the angular or other effects. It is the planet which is affected by Rahu that delivers the results.

Ketu

Just as Rahu's characteristics are similar to that of Saturn, Ketu's are similar to Mars. Therefore, as a preliminary analysis, use the information that's covered under Mars for Ketu. But again, other considerations are more important for this shadow planet, especially through the transmission of its catalytic influence on other planets. The other planets, therefore, ultimately become affected and provide Ketu's results.

7. The House Cusp Ruler - House Connection

In this chapter, the influence of a house cusp ruler on an individual by occupying a certain house is described for all house cusp rulers. Again, this information is intended to be general source material, and the specific inference and subsequent astrological interpretation will depend on several other factors as will be illustrated in the next chapter. Unless it is exclusively stated, the information provided here is only applicable if the house is occupied by a cusp ruler alone and other planets don't influence the house either by angular aspect or by the particular configuration. Usually it's very rare where the result indicated by the presence of a planet in a house doesn't get modified due to other planetary effects on that house. Unless it is explicitly stated, the reference to the masculine gender also includes the feminine gender; for example, the references to "he" and "him" also implicitly include "she" and "her."

The Ascendant Cusp Ruler

First House: When the first house cusp ruler resides in the same house the person is likely to enjoy excellent health all through his life. Overall, he is content, happy, and has tremendous faith and confidence in himself.

Second House: In the second house the ascendant cusp ruler makes one very industrious with a single goal of becoming wealthy. He may be selfish; but he earns a decent income by working hard, and he is proud of it. Usually he is the main breadwinner of the family. He has a great taste for food, and he enjoys a variety of dishes.

Third House: The person is courageous, bold, and an achiever. Usually he is successful in any endeavor he takes. He is fond of his kin; he enjoys short travel. He has a hobby that he really enjoys, which is his way of expressing himself.

Fourth House: The person is fond of his mother and vice versa. He has a happy family and home life. He is kind, compassionate, loving, and moral.

Fifth House: The person is generally an intellect. He successfully pursues higher education. He loves his children and vice versa. He enjoys travel, and usually he is perceived as a lucky person.

Sixth House: The person's resistive power against fighting viruses and germs is likely to be weak. As a result, his health is probably going to remain below normal. He is a worrisome, never contented, and a grouchy person. He is likely to suffer from failures and setbacks in his life.

Seventh House: He is likely to be dominated by his spouse. He is very adaptive, adjusting, and a flexible person. He is likely to have good business partners or supervisors at work. He is strong and he is likely to do a lot of traveling.

Eighth House:	The person is likely to be chased by diseases. In general, opportunities that present themselves to the person will be very few and far between.
Ninth House:	Overall, the person is going to be blessed with opportunities. He is fortunate to have almost anything coming to him easily. He is well liked by people; he will earn fame and social prestige. He is religious, and he is likely to spend a lot of time helping and caring for others. He is very modest and respects others. He is likely to go overseas to visit many places or migrate there.
Tenth House:	This is one of the ideal houses for the ascendant ruler to reside. The person is likely to meet all his expectations in his profession or business. He won't have trouble rising to a powerful position in the professional or business community. He believes in hard work and creativity, and has excellent interpersonal skills. If the ascendant ruler happens to be in conjunction with the tenth house ruler in the tenth house, he is likely to become a very powerful and famous person.
Eleventh House:	Financially the person is likely to do very well. He is likely to have a lot of friends and a good social life. Most of his wishes are likely to come true.
Twelfth House:	The person is likely to lack survival skills and practical knowledge. He worries a lot and is usually miserable. Opportunities don't knock on his door very often. He may be a highly opinionated type. Perhaps that makes it difficult for him to understand other's viewpoints. He may live a gypsy life, abandoning his place of birth. With unfavorable planets in the twelfth house, he is likely to end up in a jail.

The Second House Cusp Ruler

First House:	The person is extremely materialistic and selfish. He loves his family.
Second House:	The person is a true opportunist, extremely selfish, and doesn't care for others. He has sound financial stability, and he is likely to experience financial gain through an inheritance. He enjoys good and tasty food.
Third House:	The person is likely to be very talkative; he may be a writer and financially well off. Unless the second house cusp ruler is in conjunction with a malicious planet, his relationship with younger kin remains healthy. He is financially independent and is less likely to depend on anybody for anything.
Fourth House:	The person is likely to experience financial gain through a family inheritance. He is likely to spend most of his money on his family. With an inauspicious planet in the fourth house, he may get adopted or may go through experiences of living in foster homes.
Fifth House:	The person is likely to be well educated and likely to earn his living based on his educational background. He is likely to have a strong gambling interest and may gain through gambling. He is likely to spend his money on his children.
Sixth House:	The person is likely to become a victim of a scam scheme and lose money. He is likely to have a tendency toward trusting the wrong person and may take unnecessary responsibility in a high risk venture. He is likely to stay close to his maternal uncle. He is likely to experience some sudden illness which may put him in a financially difficult situation.
Seventh House:	The person's married life is likely to remain mired in problems; in particular, the spouse's expensive habits are likely to be the cause. Although, a partnership in business is beneficial, the constant occurrence of major disagreements and differences may be the cause of a breakup.

Eighth House: There is a good possibility that the person will have a sudden and unexpected financial windfall; but he would have difficulty in managing the money, and ultimately, he is likely to lose it all.

Ninth House: The second house cusp ruler in the ninth house blesses the person with continuous financial gains, and those gains are likely to further multiply if the ninth house is also occupied by the ninth house cusp ruler.

Tenth House: Financially the person will probably do very well in his business or profession. He is likely to be dealing with banks, securities, and investments conglomerates. He is likely to go into business with his father or work for him.

Eleventh House: The person has a potential to make the rank of riches. Unless the eleventh house is affected by an inauspicious planet, he is unlikely to go broke in his life.

Twelfth House: The person may make money, but the rate of its disappearance is likely to remain equally high due to unexpected incidences that he has no control over. As a result he is likely to remain in a constant state of financial worry. Also, he is likely to lose court battles and end up in serious debt. With an auspicious planet in the twelfth house, however, he is likely to be generous and donate to charities and needy institutions. With a malicious planet in the twelfth house, he needs to take care of his eyes and teeth.

The Third House Cusp Ruler

First House: The person is brave, bold, and aggressive. He is likely to be very successful in any endeavors he may himself engage in. He has realistic ambitions, he takes pride in what he does, and his relationships with his kin are likely to remain positive.

Second House: The person is likely to be thrust with the responsibility of taking care of his siblings in the early part of his life. He has a keen interest in music; he may be a good speech writer or a storyteller.

Third house: The person is courageous, bold, and strong. He loves reading. He enjoys travel, particularly short journeys. He is very analytical. His thinking is continuously affected by his surroundings and the experiences he goes through. As a result, he is a naturally fast learner. In association with an unfavorable planet in the third house, however, he could become mentally weak and unstable. He is less likely to get along with his siblings. With a favorable planet like Jupiter, Mercury, or Venus in the third house he is likely to pursue a profession that deals with writing and expressing his own ideas. With fifth house ruler in the third house, a successful career in writing is very probable.

Fourth House: The person usually enjoys a happy family life, excellent relations with his brothers and sisters, and success in higher educational pursuits. He is likely to experience a later part of his life that is very enjoyable and happy.

Fifth House: Excellent educational background! Loves and enjoys educational field. He is an intellectual with relentless curiosity and amazing grasping power for any new subject matter. He is a natural athlete and he loves to travel. His children are usually bright and make him very proud.

Sixth House: From a health standpoint, the third house cusp in the sixth house is undesirable. The person is likely to struggle to stay healthy. He is not likely to get along well with his kin. If he is a writer, he is harsh and tends to create enemies. He is likely to fall ill during travel.

Seventh House: The person has the potential to become a well known debater. He loves to take on any challenge in the area of debate and intellectual competition.

Eighth House: He is probably going to have very difficult relationships with his kin. He is likely to experience a lot of difficulties in his life.

Ninth House: The third house cusp in the ninth house makes one highly intelligent and wise. He is fortunate to have well behaved and bright children. He is always happy, and he enjoys frequent long journeys. He could become a good writer if he chooses to be one. He loves and cares for others, especially the less fortunate. He helps the poor and needy with generous donations.

Tenth House: From a professional career or business standpoint, this is an excellent placing for the third house cusp ruler. The person is likely to excel in whatever he does for a living. In addition, if the tenth house cusp ruler occupies the third house, he is likely to rise to a very high and powerful position in his social or political life.

Eleventh House: He is likely to have impressive financial gains through his brilliant and intellectual efforts. He is positively in tune with a very big network of people of high status in society. He is a true go-getter and is going to be successful in fulfilling his ambitions, goals, and desires.

Twelfth House: The person is likely to travel a long distance with his siblings. With unfavorable planets placed in the twelfth house, he is likely to unnecessarily worry about almost anything.

The Fourth House Cusp Ruler

First House: He is a happy and a friendly person. He is healthy and very fond of his mother. He is likely to design and build his own house. He is likely to do very well in his life.

Second House: Financially the person remains in great shape. He loves his family. He has a sweet voice. He is loving and caring. He is likely to earn a college degree.

Third House: The person is blessed with loving brothers and sisters that he can always count on.

Fourth House: This is one of the desirable situations in a horoscope. Depending upon the support from other planets, the person can rise to a very high position in his life. He is most likely to have all modern resources at his disposal to satisfy his personal pleasures. He is likely to be closely attached to his family. He is blessed to have a mother who really cares for and nurtures him both emotionally and physically. He is likely to do well in the field of academics.

Fifth House: The person is likely to acquire a high level of education; especially with Jupiter in the fifth house, he has tremendous potential to achieve a very high degree of success in the scientific field. He is likely to be an artist or likely to have an artistic hobby. In general, he is fortunate to have an abundance of opportunities in his life, and he is fully capable of making the most of those opportunities. With the ninth house cusp ruler in the fifth house, he is likely to become seriously interested in the religious and spiritual activities.

Sixth House: The person may have difficulty getting along with his mother, or it's likely that he lost his mother in his early childhood and he is either living with his stepmother or in a foster home. With Rahu in the sixth house, he has to deal with a serious family crisis which could take an emotional toll on him.

Seventh House: The person is likely to have a very happy marriage.

Eighth House: The person is most likely to stay unhappy. He could be in heavy debt. He probably doesn't have any family support and has to deal with the crisis all by himself. With the presence of an unfavorable planet in the eighth house (in addition to the fourth house cusp ruler), he is likely to be accident prone. He is likely to become poor in the later part of his life.

Ninth House: This is a naturally auspicious situation. The person is likely to have a great many opportunities in his life. He is likely to be very fortunate. His business or profession will expand, and he is likely to enjoy life to its fullest. He is a very religious person.

Tenth House: He is fond of his father. He is going to do extremely well in his business or profession. With either the ninth house or the ascendant cusp ruler in the tenth house he is likely to earn high social and political status; he is very ambitious, extremely self-confident, and very focused on his goals. He is very likable, highly respectable, and popular.

Eleventh House: With a planet like Jupiter or Venus in the eleventh house, the fourth house cusp ruler in this house will make the person very popular, rich, and happy. His friend circle and contacts will be very large and consist of high profile people from different walks of life.

Twelfth House: The person is likely to make a good spiritual progress. He is likely to do a lot of traveling. With the eighth house cusp ruler in the twelfth, he is likely to financially suffer, likely to lose his family and his possessions, and perhaps likely to be forced to go in exile.

The Fifth House Cusp Ruler

First House: The person is likely to be very fond of his children; he is very attached to them, and of course, very proud of them. In the field of education he is generally going to do very well. He is likely to be happy and healthy.

Second House: The person's profession is very likely to be related to the area of his education. Financially, he is going to do just fine.

Third House: The person is likely to be blessed with a powerful analytical mind, vivid imagination, and in-depth thinking. He is likely to be highly intellectual. He loves reading; he is good at writing, and has a keen interest in solving mysteries. He enjoys short travels. He has an excellent relationship with his kin.

Fourth House: The person is likely to own a house. Financially, he is likely to do well. He may pursue a career as a scientific researcher.

Fifth House: He is naturally gifted and intellectually brilliant. He may have gambling traits. His children are bright, and they make him proud.

Sixth House: The person is likely to experience delays and problems in his pursuit for education. For instance, he could become seriously ill at the time of his finals and may end up losing a semester as a result. His relationship with his children is likely to be strenuous and could become a constant source of worry.

Seventh House: The person is likely to have a lot of friends of the opposite sex. He is likely to have an excellent relationship with his spouse and a very happy marriage.

Eighth House: The person is likely to be worrisome and a bit unfortunate in his educational pursuit. The health of his children can become a source of worry. For females, having a miscarriage or a stillborn baby can be a real possibility. He is likely to experience heavy losses in gambling places and at race courses.

Ninth House: The person is likely to excel in an educational field, capturing top awards, scholarships, and fame. He is also likely to take keen interest in the spiritual field and make significant progress. He may go overseas for education, or migrate to a foreign country and settle there. His children are likely to exceed all his expectations for them. In general, he will achieve almost everything in his life. Also, he is likely to help needy people or institutions with donations. He is God fearing, and he has a strong faith in God.

Tenth House: His professional activities are likely to expand with prominent success. His profession is likely to be linked to an educational field.

Eleventh House: He is likely to have a good circle of friends he can rely on. He is very fond of his children and vice versa. Financially, he is likely to remain in an excellent state through most of his life.

Twelfth House: He is likely to be worried about his children and their future.

The Sixth House Cusp Ruler

First House: From a health standpoint, the person is likely to be weak and need to pay a lot of attention to his health. He is likely to be perceived as an unfriendly person. He may carry a birth mark on his face.

Second House: The person is likely to be unhappy with his family life. People may try to take undue advantage of him. As a result, he may find himself in a precarious situation that he cannot handle and, perhaps, run into a financial loss through his betraying friends. In other words, the people he considers his friends are likely to turn on him and destroy him. He is likely to suffer from eye and teeth problems. He will be required to provide constant medical care for his family. He may gain financially through his maternal uncles and cousins. He may experience food poisoning. He is likely to die very poor. In association with an inauspicious planet like Mars or Saturn in the second house, he is likely to be perceived as a liar, likely to get involved with the wrong people and end up behind bars.

Third House: In all likelihood, the person is mentally very unsteady and unsure. He is likely to pick a fight with his kin. He may have trouble getting along with the people around him, and he may be perceived as a jealous person.

Fourth House: At home, he is miserable and a trouble maker. He is likely to pick fights with his family members, particularly with his mother. He is likely to be accident prone. He probably doesn't have a friend he can trust.

Fifth House: The person is likely to have an attitude problem. He may even have difficulty completing basic education like a high school diploma. His children are likely to remain unhealthy, and he is likely to have a poor relationship with them.

Sixth House: The person is likely to enjoy pleasures in life. His maternal uncle is likely to help him get started in his life. He is healthy, and likely to do well in his profession. He may pursue his profession in the field of medicine and surgery.

Seventh House: It would be very difficult for him to get along with his spouse and business partners, if he has any. His social reputation is likely to get tarnished due to his alleged involvement and affairs with other women. He is likely to lose important battles in his life.

Eighth House: The person may experience a variety of diseases in his lifetime. Usually he has difficulty getting along with any of his relatives.

Ninth House: The person is likely to face his life with almost no opportunities. He is likely to lack self respect and confidence in himself. He is likely to be an atheist.

Tenth House: He is unlikely to do well in his chosen profession. He probably has a problem getting along with his father.

Eleventh House: His friends are untrustworthy! Often he is likely to be cheated by his friends. Financially he is likely to stay unhappy, always complaining. His relationships with his children are likely sour.

Twelfth House: He has a natural tendency to make enemies. He is likely to stay worried about his health. He may have an eye disease or a foot problem. With the presence of an inauspicious planet in the twelfth house of his horoscope, he could become possessed, turn into a mentally retarded person, or have a part of his body permanently paralyzed.

The Seventh House Cusp Ruler

First House: The spouse is likely to dominate the person. He usually backs down in the marriage and lets the spouse lead.

Second House: Financial gains are likely to materialize through dealings with a person of the opposite sex, and also after marriage. In association with an undesirable planet in the second house, his marriage is likely to suffer a setback; the spouse may become seriously ill. He may lose a court battle.

Third House: The person enjoys his short travels. With an auspicious planet in the third house, his spouse brings luck in their married life. In association with a malicious planet in the third house, he is likely to pick a fight with his kin brothers and sisters. He has a vascillating personality and may be unsteady in his actions.

Fourth House: The person is likely to be happy in his marriage. He loves and cares for his spouse. He is likely to have a good relationship with his in-laws.

Fifth House: The person is likely to go through a series of relationships before his marriage. He and his spouse are very compatible with each other, and as a result, they are likely to be very happy in their marriage. The spouse is likely to be interested in arts, music, drama, opera, or he (or she) could himself (herself) be an artist. With Venus in the seventh house he may go to an extreme in his sexual endeavors.

Sixth House: It becomes a challenge for both spouses to keep their relationship reasonably sound. Misunderstanding, miscommunication, and misinformation occur routinely, and in general, their individual characteristics have a natural tendency to be not very complementary with each other. That leaves very little room for reconciliation. The spouse may become seriously ill, and the illness may last for a long time. In the presence of an inauspicious planet in the sixth house, the matter gets worse. The spouses may turn against each other as enemies.

Seventh House: It brings happiness in marriage, and the marriage lasts long.

Eighth House: There is always something lacking that is needed for his marriage chemistry to work. The spouse is likely to become ill with a chronic disease.

Ninth House: In all likelihood, immediately after the person's wedding, his luck begins to shine. He begins to get breaks in his life that he has been waiting for or was denied before. He is likely to travel, perhaps a long distance, and visit far away places. He enjoys his marriage, and deeply cares for and loves his spouse.

Tenth House: The spouse is very active, has self-pride, is understanding and smart. Financially, the spouse is likely to make a big contribution in the marriage.

Eleventh House: The person has more friends of the opposite sex, and with their help he is likely to do financially very well in his life. He is likely to be very social, an extrovert, and popular in his friend circle.

Twelfth House: The person is likely to get drawn into a fight or quarrel with others due to his spouse. He is likely to get his name tarnished or his prestige destroyed in the process. The marriage is pretty much a rollercoaster ride. A long spousal illness, misunderstanding, and cheating is likely to occur frequently, causing more problems. He may be a heavy gambler and likely to lose a lot in gambling.

The Eighth House Cusp Ruler

First House: The person may be physically weak, with a poor immune system to resist viral attacks. With an inauspicious planet in the first house, he may become handicapped due to a severe accident.

Second House: From a financial standpoint, the more a person makes money the faster he loses it. He may have to assume financial responsibility for his parents at a very early age, incurring unexpected and unmanageable expenses. He may have his eyes and teeth inflicted with diseases. In the presence of the ascendant ruler or the eleventh house cusp ruler in the second house, he may experience a financial windfall, perhaps through acquiring an inheritance.

Third House: His relationships with his brothers and sisters (especially younger ones) remain strained. Mentally, he may become weak. He may become so pessimistic about his life that he is likely to think about attempting suicide. He may experience an early hearing loss.

Fourth House: The person is likely to remain unhappy in his life. He may lose his mother early in his life. He probably has to go through an unexpected hardship in his life. He is likely to be denied a reasonable family life.

Fifth House: Females are likely to experience abnormalities in their maternal deliveries. They may have to go through an experience like having a miscarriage or a still born baby. The child may have some physical birth defect. Happiness from children and vice versa would be very rare. He may become mentally unstable, and may get admitted to an asylum as a result. He is likely to fail in his love affairs.

Sixth House: From a health standpoint, the person is likely to go through a very difficult time.

Seventh House: The person is likely to have unpleasant surprises and disappointments in his marriage.

Eighth House: The person is likely to see a totally unexpected financial windfall, either through an inheritance, by winning a lottery, or having a very lucky day at the race course.

Ninth House: Despite his capabilities the person is likely to be denied opportunities in his life. He is likely to face unfortunate situations in his life which are perhaps unfair.

Tenth House: The person's relationship with his father is likely to remain poor and unhealthy. Also, his progress in his profession or business is likely to stay below average. In his profession, he is likely to experience difficulty in getting along with his superiors and colleagues. His business may incur a big financial loss.

Eleventh House: At least for some time in his life, the person is likely to do very well financially. He may experience difficulty getting along with his friends. He may lose his dearest friend.

Twelfth House: The person is likely to be burdened with family responsibilities, financial worries, and anxieties. He may be faced with frequent unexpected financial losses. He may become bankrupt.

The Ninth House Cusp Ruler

First House: The person is likely to be a perfect gentleman, loving, caring, and compassionate. Luck is likely to stay with him for a good part of his life. He is likely to stay in excellent health. He may be a very religious person.

Second House: The person is likely to remain in an excellent financial condition. He is likely to make frequent donations to help the needy!

Third House: The relationship with his brothers and sisters is likely to be very positive and beneficial. He enjoys travel; being creative, he is likely to have a strong interest in writing. He is also an articulator. He is likely to be raised in a healthy environment with positive reinforcement. He is likely to be perceived as a highly amiable and respected person in society.

Fourth House: The person is likely to be blessed with a happy family life. He sets a definite goal in his life, and he is very likely to achieve it. He is a peace loving and a perfect gentleman. He is likely to be adored by his fellow man.

Fifth House: The person is likely to pursue a career in an educational field. He has tremendous potential to be a researcher, and he has enough patience and stamina to become a successful one in any field he chooses. He is likely to become a well known authority in his field. He has a natural interest in philosophy, psychology, religion and spiritual areas. He is likely to go overseas for education. He is likely to become a good role model for students.

Sixth House: The person is likely to receive an improper consultation resulting in a financial loss or a damaged reputation.

Seventh House: The person is likely to enjoy his life to its fullest immediately after his wedding. He is lucky to get married with an ideal spouse. His spouse is likely to encourage him in all of his endeavors and provide the necessary support to make him successful. He is likely to be associated with good business partners or colleagues in his profession.

Eighth House: The person is likely to suffer from a series of setbacks in his life. He is likely to have very few opportunities and more obstacles in his life.

Ninth House: The person is considered to be very fortunate. He is likely to get whatever he wants in his life. Popularity, fame, wealth, and social prestige are likely to follow him. He has the potential to become a very famous and rich person.

Tenth House: The person is likely to do very well in his profession. He is very fond of his father and vice versa. His intuitive abilities are excellent. He seldom errs in his judgment. He is likely to achieve his goals in a very short time.

Eleventh House: The person is likely to become very wealthy and is likely to enjoy all material pleasures in his life.

Twelfth House: From a material progress standpoint, the ninth house cusp ruler in the twelfth house denies happiness to the person. However, he has the potential to make tremendous progress in the spiritual field. He is likely to travel to far away places to pursue his philosophical and religious interests.

The Tenth House Cusp Ruler

First House: The person is likely to be very dynamic, active, and a true achiever. His interpersonal skills are remarkable. He is ambitious; he has a tremendous drive, stamina, and patience. As a result, he is likely to become a successful leader, manager, or an officer with a high level of responsibility.

Second House: The person is likely to exceed all his financial expectations in his profession or business. His profession is likely to deal with banks, financial institutions, treasury departments, and securities exchanges. He may pursue a career in successfully running restaurants and hotels.

Third House: The person is very independent, bold, and positive; he is likely to take on a challenge on his own and be successful. He is ambitious, and a true go-getter. He is brave, and usually achieves his goal.

Fourth House: He is likely to succeed in anything he does. He loves and adores his family. He is homesick, and does a lot of things for his family. He enjoys life as best as he can.

Fifth House: The person is likely to make a great progress in education. He is likely to pursue a career in either an educational field or in arts or sports.

Sixth House: The person is likely to have a good job, and he is likely to do well. His subordinates are likely to be very loyal to him and trustworthy.

Seventh House: The person is likely to be lucky in his profession. He would win over his competitors.

Eighth House: The person is likely to have a very strenuous relationship with his father as well as with his colleagues in his profession. He is likely to experience unexpected delays in his work.

Ninth House: The person is likely to be very famous in his profession. He will earn social prestige, an envious reputation, and high regard. He is likely to help others, and care for them.

Tenth House: The person is likely to be very fond of his father and vice versa. His father is likely to have a very good social reputation and a lot of wealth. With Jupiter in the tenth house, he is likely to do exceedingly well in whatever endeavor he pursues.

Eleventh House: The person is likely to make a lot of money in his profession.

Twelfth House: The person is likely to suffer heavy losses and disappointments in his business. He is likely to be consumed by his worries about his frequent failures in his profession or business.

The Eleventh House Cusp Ruler

First House: The person is likely to make a decent living by his own efforts and hard work. He is unlikely to have a financial worry. To him money usually comes easily.

Second House: The person is likely to have a heavy financial gain, especially through a family inheritance. Also, he is very capable of managing his money. He has a natural tendency to make a good investment decision. He is likely to enjoy a variety of tasty foods.

Third House: The person is likely to earn a decent living. He is likely to help his brothers and sisters financially.

Fourth House: The person is likely to own real estate. He usually has a few good friends. He loves his family; he enjoys his life with whatever he has, and he is usually content.

Fifth House: The person is likely to achieve his educational ambition and goal. He is very fond of his children. They usually have very happy times together. He also has a large friend circle that he enjoys. He likes to gamble every now and then, and he usually wins. He loves sports, art, music, and other entertainment activities.

Sixth House: His friends cheat on him. He is likely to suffer financial losses due to taking undue responsibility for others and trusting the wrong people.

Seventh House: The person is likely to financially benefit from colleagues of the opposite sex and from his spouse as well.

Eighth House: The person is likely to experience a sudden financial windfall in his life. However, with a planet like Mars or Uranus in the eighth house, he is likely to suffer from a series of financial setbacks in his life.

Ninth House: Financially, the person's position is likely to remain extremely sound all through his life. In addition, with a planet like Jupiter, Venus, or Moon in the ninth house he is likely to become very wealthy. He is very generous and helps the needy.

Tenth House: The person is justly rewarded for his efforts in his profession or business. He is likely to do very well in whatever profession he chooses. He is likely to be very satisfied with his achievements in his life.

Eleventh House: The person is likely to be social and a real extrovert. He is likely to have a large friend circle and network of contacts. He himself is well educated, and his children are likely to do well in their lives.

Twelfth House: The person is likely to experience a financial crisis despite his decent earning power. Somehow he lacks the ability to manage his money and is also likely to make poor investment decisions which could result in serious losses.

The Twelfth House Cusp Ruler

First House: The person is likely to be worried about his health. He may be mentally weak. If the ascendant cusp ruler gets placed in the twelfth house, he is likely to lose everything he has and is likely to spend a good part of his life in a prison or in a confined place. He is likely to be consumed with serious worries.

Second House: The person starts his life with a heavy loan or debt and ends up spending a good part of his life repaying the loan or clearing the debt. He is likely to get involved in situations where he, sometimes unnecessarily, ends up assuming financial responsibilities for others. In general, he is not likely to enjoy material happiness and he is likely to remain poor.

Third House: The person is likely to make long journeys and visit far away places. He may leave his place of birth and migrate to a far away country to start a new life. He is an introvert and a pessimist.

Fourth House: He is likely to remain unhappy, always complaining about little things. His home life is likely to be very disappointing.

Fifth House: His ambition of completing a degree in education may get hampered or delayed by unforeseen problems over which he has no control. Perhaps he may not be able to pursue his educational ambition due to a lack of financial support. He is likely to worry about his children and their problems. His children may cause him anguish.

Sixth House: His adversaries are likely to be a constant source of headache for him. He is likely to be misunderstood by people surrounding him. He may get inflicted with a serious disease, and could end up spending a lot of time in a hospital.

Seventh House: His marriage is likely to begin on the wrong foot, and the spousal relationship is likely to remain strenuous. A person of the opposite sex may become responsible for fights and quarrels that he is likely to experience in his life. He is likely to keep the wrong company of people.

Eighth House: Health may become a major cause of concern in his life. He may have to bear with a hardship for quite a while before things turn for the better.

Ninth House: From a material pleasure standpoint, this configuration is probably undesirable. The person is likely to stay aloof and away from the places of action and activities. He may become a hermit. On a spiritual level he may make good progress.

Tenth House: The person is likely to face a series of obstacles, delays, and misfortunes in his professional activities. He is likely to have trouble staying focused in his profession. His actions are likely to be the result of his vascillating nature. He is likely to be consumed by his business or professional worries. He is likely to get insulted, defeated, and may have to face the inevitable downfall.

Eleventh House: The person is likely to be burdened with financial worries. His friends are likely to desert him. He may get involved with the wrong company of people, causing himself a lot of anguish as a result.

Twelfth House: In association with an auspicious planet like Jupiter or Venus in the twelfth house, he is likely to have opportunities in his life of which he can make use. He is likely to be religious, inward, and have a natural tendency to help others. However, in the presence of a malicious planet like Mars or Uranus in the twelfth house, he may face frequent adverse situations in his life. He may suddenly lose all he has. His eyes may become inflicted with a disease, and he may develop a problem with his feet.

8. Analysis / Interpretation

In this chapter, Mr. Nixon's horoscope is analyzed to illustrate the eastern (fixed zodiac) system based horoscope analysis procedure. For the analysis many aspects are considered, and where appropriate detailed explanations are provided. It is important to recognize that it is dangerous to rush to conclusions until all aspects are carefully considered. In particular, an assessment of the strength of a planet is the key step in a horoscope interpretation. It requires an in-depth analysis of the combined (aspects, angles, influence through the zodiac signs as well as houses) effects of all the planets, the houses planets reside in and the zodiac signs they occupy. Also, the analysis provides the insight for a person's potential talents and capabilities that he can realize if he so wishes, as well as his limitations, the awareness of which he can use to his advantage.

The analysis steps are as follows.

Referring to the horoscope illustrated in Figure 5.2, the very first thing is to look at the distribution of the planets in the zodiac as below.

I.

Fire signs:	There are four planets which occupy the fire signs: Mars, Mercury, Jupiter, and the Sun. They all fall in the sign of Sagittarius.
Earth signs:	Saturn in Taurus, Ketu (Moon's descending node) in Virgo, and Moon and Uranus in Capricorn. Thus, there are four planets in the earth signs.
Air signs:	Pluto in Gemini and Venus in Aquarius make a total of two planets in air signs.
Water signs:	The remaining two planets, Neptune and Rahu (ascending lunar node) belong to Cancer and Pisces respectively.

The preliminary observation: In his life Mr. Nixon might have experienced a lot of action oriented events (four planets in the fire signs) and been part of a hard working environment with a great deal of material success (four planets in the earth signs).

2.

Dynamic signs:	Aries, Cancer, Libra, and Capricorn are the dynamic (constantly on the move) signs. Three planets—Neptune, Uranus and Moon—occupy these signs.
Fixed signs:	Taurus, Leo, Scorpio, and Aquarius are the fixed (determined, strong willed, and focused) signs. Saturn and Venus belong to these signs.
Flexible signs:	Gemini, Virgo, Sagittarius, and Pisces are the flexible (dual in nature, adaptive, unsure) signs. All the remaining seven planets fall in these signs.

The preliminary observation: The planetary dominance in the flexible signs means Mr. Nixon might not be very decisive. However, he might be very receptive to looking at other's points of view and would probably make constant adjustments to his decision making process as he sees fit.

3.

The planet Jupiter resides in the zodiac sign it rules. In other words, Jupiter is in its own sign. The more planets there are that occupy the signs they rule, the stronger the horoscope becomes. Also, Jupiter is the owner of the fifth house and the eighth house since cusps of these houses fall in the signs Sagittarius and Pisces respectively. While the planet Mars doesn't belong to the zodiac sign it rules (Aries and Scorpio are ruled by Mars), it resides in its own house as the fourth house cusp falls in the sign of Scorpio.

The planets Saturn and Venus occupy each other's signs (Taurus is ruled by Venus while Saturn rules the sign of Aquarius). This is considered an important configuration since the tenth and seventh houses are involved in this exchange. When planets exchange each other's signs, the combined qualities of the planets strengthen the horoscope manyfold for the areas signified by the houses to which the planets belong. According to Parashara, the noted Indian astrologer who provided the basic foundation for astrology some three thousand years ago, "When the tenth house cusp ruler falls in the zodiac sign owned by the seventh house cusp ruler, and at the same time no evil (or unfavorable) planet aspects the tenth house cusp ruler, the person has the potential to become the king of kings." For the twentieth century, it can be interpreted as a person who is profoundly capable of affecting world affairs.

The planets Pluto, Neptune, and Saturn are retrograde. The effects of the retrograde planets in terms of their influence on an individual has been an important topic of debate among the astrologers. It is my experience that the favorable effects of retrograde planets during their active cycles can be fully materialized only when they are retrograde during their active cycles and vice-versa. The details of the active cycles are dealt with in Part II, Chapters 10 and 11.

4.

So far interrelationships between planets and zodiac signs, planets and planets have been analyzed. The next step is to note a planetary position with respect to the cusp of its house. In other words, determine how many degrees a planet is away from its house cusp. The closer it is to the cusp, the stronger its influence becomes. In Mr. Nixon's horoscope, Sun and Moon are right on their respective house cusps.

The preliminary observation: Sun being the ascendant ruler positioned at the fifth house cusp made Mr. Nixon extremely powerful in dealing with the public. However, Moon, the ruler of the twelfth house, on the sixth house cusp created an uncomfortable situation when he had to deal with his adversaries. Moon represents mind, the sixth house enemies, and the twelfth house the loss or transformation. In essence, it all adds up to a constant struggle when it comes to dealing with the public.

5. The Planetary Angles:

In Mr. Nixon's horoscope planetary angles are as follows:

Conjunction:	Mars-Mercury, Mars-Jupiter, and Mercury-Jupiter, all in the fourth house
Semi-sextile:	Sun-Moon, Jupiter-Uranus, Venus-Uranus, Saturn-Pluto
Sextile:	Jupiter-Venus
Quincunx:	Mars-Saturn, Mercury-Saturn, Uranus-Pluto
Opposition:	Mars-Pluto, Mercury-Pluto, Jupiter-Pluto

Preliminary Inference: There are no trines and only one sextile angle. There are three quincunx (150°) angles, which very likely caused the onset of difficult and challenging situations in Mr. Nixon's life, especially during the periods when the negative influence of Saturn, Mars, Uranus, or Pluto was operative. The three angles of conjunctions are beneficial in the fourth house. But the most important ones, in my opinion, are the three oppositions which are responsible for bringing out the best in Mr. Nixon as far as his political life was concerned. Later, in discussing the ninefold horoscope of Mr. Nixon, this inference will become more apparent.

6. Planetary Effects

One planet can affect the other planets through their respective house positions. For example, in Mr. Nixon's horoscope, Neptune is in the eleventh house. The fifth house being directly opposite of the eleventh, Neptune affects the planets in the fifth house. Thus, Neptune is said to affect the Sun and Uranus. Since every planet affects the planets residing in its opposite house, the planets Uranus and Sun also affect the planet Neptune (being in the house opposite of the fifth house). For a planetary affect, it is not important to consider the zodiac sign to which the planet belongs, but the houses in which the planet resides.

In addition to affecting the planets in the directly opposite house, some planets influence planets in other houses. Those are:

Jupiter: In addition to affecting the planets in the directly opposite house, Jupiter affects planets in the houses that are fifth and ninth from its house. The house counting begins from the house in which the planet resides. In Mr. Nixon's horoscope, Jupiter is in the fourth house. Therefore, it affects planets in the eighth house and the twelfth house in addition to the planets in the tenth house. Although there are no planets in the eighth and twelfth houses, Jupiter still positively modifies the results signified by the eighth and twelfth houses due to its beneficial influence.

Mars: Mars affects planets in the houses that are fourth and eighth from its house. In Mr. Nixon's horoscope, Mars being in the fourth house, affects the houses seventh, tenth, and eleventh and planets in those houses. Thus, Mars affects Rahu (seventh house resident), Pluto (tenth house resident), and Neptune (eleventh house resident). By nature Mars is regarded as a malicious planet, and, therefore, its effect is negative. However, in Mr. Nixon's horoscope, Mars being in conjunction with Jupiter (an auspicious planet), its negative effect is considerably reduced.

Saturn: Saturn eyes planets in the houses that are third and tenth from its house in addition to the seventh house (directly opposite as described earlier) from its own house. In Mr. Nixon's chart, Saturn resides in the ninth house. Therefore, it affects the eleventh house (third from the ninth) and the planet Neptune, the third house (seventh from the ninth), the sixth house (tenth from the ninth) and the planets Venus and Moon occupying the sixth house. In general, Saturn, being a malicious planet, affects unfavorably.

7. The House-Planet Connection:

Referring to Chapter 6: "The House-Planet Connection," the significance of a planet occupying a particular house can be summarized as follows.

Sun in the fifth house:

Mr. Nixon probably had a tendency to act up. With the auspicious Neptune in the eleventh house affecting the fifth house Sun, he completed his degree in higher education; he probably was fond of his children.

Moon in the sixth house:

In this house Moon makes the person feel suffocated. He is always likely to blame others or situations that he is unable to handle. The sixth house being the tenth from the ninth house, the ninth house Saturn affects the sixth house. However, Saturn's influence is likely to be more positive than negative for it rules the sixth house.

Mercury in the fourth house:

Mercury is in conjunction with Mars and Jupiter in the fourth house. Although Mars in the fourth house is not desirable, the presence of Jupiter in the fourth house is very positive. As a result, Mercury makes the person loving, talkative and happy. He probably had a lot of good friends and relations. He tended to get homesick often and probably remained very attached to his mother.

Venus in the sixth house:

It is not a happy situation to have Venus in the sixth house. Although capable, Mr. Nixon never had a chance to have his artistic abilities developed. Typical qualities of this Venus are notorious, weird, lazy, antisocial, unhappy, and some flaw in character.

Mars in the fourth house:

Mars alone in the fourth house without any positive support from other planets either through association, angle, or aspect creates a turbulent atmosphere in the home (family) life. But with the planet Jupiter in the fourth house, the unfavorable influence of Mars is considerably diminished. Mr. Nixon's mother had a strong positive influence on him.

Jupiter in the fourth house:

The general tendency for this Jupiter is to create and maintain happy surroundings against all odds. He generally has a good family life. He is likely to be closely attached to his mother.

Saturn in the ninth house:

The ninth house Saturn made Mr. Nixon orthodox and ultra conservative. He was generally intelligent, just, and very patient. He had the potential to become a lawyer, a religious authority, or a research scientist.

Uranus in the fifth house:

This house provides proper nourishment for Uranus's intellectual capabilities. All by itself, Uranus is probably not that effective in this house, but with Sun in the fifth house Uranus made Mr. Nixon extraordinarily powerful. He pursued political challenges and thrived on them. As a part of his personality he was a true gambler.

Neptune in the eleventh house:

This Neptune might have caused Mr. Nixon unnecessary delays in financial matters that perhaps mostly resulted in losses. He placed too much confidence in the friends who would not go along with him. He might have been in the company of the wrong people.

Rahu in the seventh house:

The person with Rahu in the seventh house usually gets married late. Usually married life is not very high on the person's priority list.

Ketu in the first house:

Ketu in the first house made Mr. Nixon very energetic and strong. He was tall. He was impatient, impulsive, aggressive, and an ambitious person. He was confident, determined, insistent, hardworking, very independent, and a true self-starter. Anger and perhaps revenge might have been his biggest weaknesses. But he never let up. He loved power; he loved to command others; he had a natural inclination for politics and national leadership to exercise his authority and power.

9. The House Cusp Ruler-House Connection

The ascendant cusp ruler in the fifth house:

The person is generally an intellect. He successfully pursues higher education. He loves his children and vice versa. He enjoys travel, and usually he is perceived as a lucky person.

The second house cusp ruler in the fourth house:

The person is likely to experience financial gain through a family inheritance. He is likely to spend most of his money on his family. With an inauspicious planet in the fourth house, he may get adopted or may go through experiences of living in a foster home.

The third house cusp ruler in the sixth house:

From a health standpoint, the third house cusp in the sixth house is undesirable. The person is likely to struggle to stay healthy. He is not likely to get along well with his kin. If he is a writer, he is harsh and tends to create enemies. He is likely to fall ill during travel.

The fourth house cusp ruler in the fourth house:

This is one of the desirable situations in a horoscope. Depending upon the support from other planets, the person can rise to a very high position in his life. He is most likely to have all modern resources at his disposal to satisfy his personal pleasures. He is likely to be closely attached to his family. He is blessed to have a mother who really cares for and nurtures him both emotionally and physically. He is likely to do well in the field of academics.

The fifth house cusp ruler in the fourth house:

The person is likely to own a house. Financially, he is likely to do well.

The sixth house cusp ruler in the ninth house:

He is likely to lack self-respect and confidence in himself. He is likely to be an atheist.

The seventh house cusp ruler in the ninth house:

In all likelihood, immediately after the person's wedding his luck begins to shine. He begins to get breaks in his life that he has been waiting for or was denied before. He is likely to travel, perhaps a long distance, and visit far away places with his spouse.

The eighth house cusp ruler in the fourth house:

The person is likely to remain unhappy in his life. He may lose his mother early in his life. He probably has to go through an unexpected hardship in his life. He is likely to be denied a reasonable family life.

The ninth house cusp ruler in the fourth house:

The person is likely to be blessed with a happy family life. He sets a definite goal in his life, and he is very likely to achieve it. He is peace loving and a perfect gentleman. He is likely to be adored by his fellow man.

The tenth house cusp ruler in the sixth house:

The person is likely to have a good job, and he is likely to do well. His subordinates are likely to be very loyal and trustworthy to him.

The eleventh house cusp ruler in the fourth house:

The person is likely to own real estate. He usually has a few good friends. He loves his family; he enjoys his life with whatever he has, and he is usually content.

The twelfth house cusp ruler in the sixth house:

His adversaries are likely to be a constant source of headache for him. He is likely to be misunderstood by people surrounding him. He may get inflicted with a serious disease and could end up spending a lot of time in a hospital.

From the general house-planet and the cusp ruler-house connection information as listed above for Mr. Nixon's horoscope, notice that there are cases where one set of information appears to be in direct contradiction with another set. For instance, as per the eighth house cusp ruler in the fourth house, Mr. Nixon is likely to remain unhappy in his life; however, the ninth house cusp ruler in the fourth house provided him with the blessing of a happy family life. Actually both statements are true if understood in the proper context. At a given time, a certain planet's influence is usually more prominent than others, and as a result a person's unique experience in his life is tied to that particular planet's influence on him during that period causing him to have that experience. At another time, one of the other planets' dominant influence may take him in the direction providing him with exactly the opposite type of experience. In Part II, the justification of this apparent paradox is provided on the basis of planetary cycles.

In summary, the essence of Mr. Nixon's horoscope is:

The unique placing of Uranus, Neptune, and Pluto made his horoscope tremendously important. As pointed out earlier, the planet Pluto provided a tremendous boost for Mars, Mercury, and Jupiter through the direct opposition angle (180 degrees) to bring out the "best" in him. The powerful Uranus in the fifth house with Sun being on the cusp gave him the ability and energy to lead the world. The auspicious Neptune in the eleventh house helped him rise to the top with the successful dialogue and dealing with communist China.

The placing of Moon on the sixth house cusp had created a very uncomfortable situation for him in dealing with his adversaries. Astrologically Mr. Nixon's political downfall cannot be linked more accurately than with the unique placing of Moon in his horoscope.

9. The Ninefold Horoscope

The concept of the ninefold horoscope of a natal chart is not new. It has been in use, particularly in India where it originated several hundred years ago, but not always with success. Its limited success, perhaps, may be attributed to its improper use without really understanding the principle behind its application.

The ninefold horoscope of a natal chart, in essence, provides a microscopic view of the natal chart and helps in assessing the planetary strength. In other words, a planet may have an excellent place in the natal chart with respect to the house it occupies and the zodiac sign it belongs to. In addition, it may be placed favorably to receive positive energies of other planets. But if that planet doesn't get placed favorably in the ninefold horoscope, the degree of confidence in realizing the predictions offered solely on the basis of the natal chart analysis, as presented earlier, can be drastically reduced.

What follows is the description of steps for generating the ninefold horoscope for a given natal chart:

- Note the ascendant position in the natal chart. Convert it in degrees away from the starting point (zero degrees of Aries) of the zodiac based on the Eastern zodiac system.

  Using Mr. Nixon's natal chart as an example, the ascendant falls on 24° and 45' of Leo. Therefore, ascendant degrees = 144° - 45'

- Calculate the ninefold ascendant position by multiplying the ascendant degrees by the number 9, and if the value exceeds 360° subtract 360° or a multiple of 360° from the value until it reduces to a number that lies between 0° and 360°.

  Thus, the ninefold ascendant degrees for Mr. Nixon's natal chart = 1332° - 45' or
  $$= 1332° - 45' - 1080$$
  $$= 222° - 45'$$

  Therefore, the ninefold ascendant is 12° - 45' of Scorpio.

- Similarly calculate the ninefold zodiac positions for all the planets.

- Cast the ninefold horoscope with the ninefold ascendant as calculated above and place all the planets as per their ninefold zodiac positions. Note that there are no house cusp positions for the ninefold horoscope. The ninefold planetary positions are shown in Table 9.1.

Since a difference beyond three degrees between two planets in conjunction places them in the adjacent zodiac signs in the ninefold horoscope, a pair of planets that are considered as making a certain angle (usually the conjunction and a multiple of thirty degree angle, as described earlier in Chapter 3) needs to be within three degrees of that angle.

The ninefold horoscope for Mr. Nixon's fixed zodiac system based natal chart is shown in Figure 9.1. The ninefold planetary positions shown in the figure are rounded off to the nearest quarter of a degree.

Table 9.1

Planets	Ninefold Zodiac Position
Ascendant	Scorpio 12° - 45'
Sun	Sagittarius 1° - 39'
Moon	Virgo 7° - 56'
Mars	Gemini 4° - 48'
Mercury	Gemini 7° - 11'
Jupiter	Gemini 22° - 12'
Venus	Capricorn 8° - 23'
Saturn	Aquarius 14° - 33'
Uranus	Aries 1° - 12'
Neptune	Cancer 19° - 57'
Pluto	Scorpio 24° - 54'
Rahu	Scorpio 12° - 18'
Ketu	Taurus 12° - 18'

Before assessing the strength of each planet in light of the ninefold horoscope of Mr. Nixon's natal chart, some general observations are noted as follows.

The ascendant of the natal chart is Leo ruled by Sun, while the ascendant of the ninefold horoscope is Scorpio ruled by Mars. Both of these planets in the natal chart reside in the fire sign Sagittarius. That explains why Mr. Nixon was a true warrior, very stubborn, and secretive as signified by the Scorpio ascendant in his ninefold natal horoscope.

In addition, the positions of the planets in the ninefold horoscope reveal quite a bit of information. For instance, the ascendant ruler Mars also occupies the secretive eighth house in a very close association with Mercury. Perhaps this may be one of the reasons why it was difficult for people to understand him. Other information as revealed by his ninefold natal chart is covered as we begin to assess the strength of each individual planet based on its position in both the natal and the ninefold natal horoscopes.

First of all, note the placing of the lunar nodes in the ninefold horoscope. Rahu is placed right on the ascendant cusp. In my opinion with this placement Rahu is the strongest responsible planet in bestowing the world's highest political power to Mr. Nixon. Rahu's effects in terms of the results it offers are closer to that of Saturn. Ascendant Rahu's typical characteristics are extremely industrious, possessive, very ambitious, selfish and self-centered. It makes one very famous, wealthy, and powerful. However, Rahu in the ascendant also means a flaw in the person's character.

Next to Rahu is the planet Pluto which occupies the first house of the ninefold chart. Recall the influence of the tenth house Pluto in the natal chart providing the tremendous amount of energy to the planets Mars, Jupiter, and Mercury through the opposition angles. The Pluto in the ninefold ascendant is extremely important

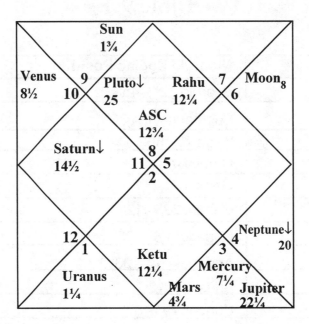

The ninefold horoscope of Mr. Nixon's natal chart.

—Figure 9.1—

in materializing the global transformation processes that are initiated by someone like the President of the United States. The power of the tenth house Pluto in the natal chart signifying the political dealing is tremendously enhanced by its placement in the ascendant of the ninefold natal chart to carry out the vision that Mr. Nixon had especially in the international arena.

The planet Neptune which occupies the eleventh house in the natal chart is placed in the most auspicious ninth house in the ninefold horoscope making him immensely lucky in having Mr. Kissinger as his foreign policy advisor and in successful endeavors dealing with communist regions like China and the Soviet Union.

The fifth house Uranus of his birth chart is placed in the sixth house of the ninefold natal chart giving Mr. Nixon the power that he needed to deal with his adversaries. This Uranus was responsible for giving him many political victories here at home and abroad as well. However, interestingly, as the characteristics of the planet Uranus are very close to those of the United States as a nation, and especially Washington D. C. as a city, it's no surprise that Mr. Nixon's adversaries who were responsible for his political downfall came from inside the beltway.

Notice that the modern planets Pluto, Neptune, and Uranus which are referred as the ambassadors of the galaxies are all well placed (perhaps with the exception of Uranus to some extent) in Mr. Nixon's chart.

Next is Sun which is responsible for providing the leadership qualities. It occupies the second house of the ninefold chart. In the natal chart, being the ruler of the ascendant occupying the fifth house in the fire sign Sagittarius, it becomes exalted as it also resides in the same zodiac sign in the ninefold chart. In addition, being the tenth house ruler of the ninefold horoscope it becomes tremendously powerful to realize the highest political office in the world and to provide the global leadership.

The placing of Jupiter and Mars in the eighth house of the ninefold horoscope make them somewhat weak as the eighth house is unsuitable for them. But the strength of Mercury is enhanced by its occupancy in the favorable eighth house. Further the positive influence of Sun from the second house of the ninefold chart has made Mercury more powerful.

There is nothing exceptional about the placement of the planets Venus and Saturn. While the weaker sixth house Venus, with its negative influence in the natal chart, is somewhat reduced by its placement in the third house of the ninefold chart, the strength of the ninth house Saturn in the natal chart is adversely affected by its weak positioning in the fourth house of the ninefold chart.

The weakest sixth house Moon in the natal chart, as discussed earlier in the previous section, is luckily placed in the eleventh house in the ninefold natal chart. As a result, the negative effect of the sixth house Moon is considerably reduced making him successful in winning the bid for the White House after losing the first time in 1960.

In general, Venus, Moon, Mercury, and Saturn seem to be less powerful, perhaps weak in providing Mr. Nixon with the positive influence in his political career.

Part II: When?

10. The Planetary Cycles

In the first part of this book, astrology was introduced with the idea that the reader had very little or no previous exposure to astrology. Starting from our solar system the unique characteristics of the planets, Sun, Moon, and the lunar nodes Rahu and Ketu were briefly described. The focus was on the salient features of each one of them. Next the concept of the zodiac, along with the precession of the equinoxes and the division of the zodiac in twelve equal parts resulting in the familiar twelve zodiac signs was presented. After a brief description of the significance and the characteristics that are attributed to each of these zodiac signs, the concept of a horoscope with its twelve houses was introduced. Next the significance of each of these twelve houses was discussed. Using Mr. Nixon's birth information as an example, a horoscope casting procedure was explained in detail.

As a basis for analyzing and interpreting a horoscope from the interrelationships among the planets themselves, the respective zodiac signs and the houses the planets occupy, and the influence of the house cusp rulers and their intricate connections to other planets through angles and the zodiac signs were provided. Analysis and interpretation of Mr. Nixon's horoscope was used to illustrate the interrelationships among the planets as well as among the planets and houses and the zodiac signs. Finally, the ninefold horoscope concept was presented. Again using Mr. Nixon's natal chart as an example, the assessment of planetary strength was presented based on the combined analysis of both the natal and its ninefold chart.

The discussion of an interpretation of a horoscope as provided in the first part, using Mr. Nixon's natal chart as an example, dealt extensively with various aspects of an individual's life. These may include personality, education, career, profession, business, money matters, relationships, marriages, family life, children, travel, good times, spiritual trends, and religious activities. In addition, the first part dealt with the degree of success a person can have in a particular endeavor. The next obvious question is when—when is a certain thing likely to happen in a person's life?

This part presents the details on "when" those predictions are likely to be realized.

The underlining concept in the application of planetary cycles in arriving at the possible time period during which a certain event is most likely to occur is that when a certain planet's cycle is operative, the predictions offered by that planet are very likely to be realized during that time.

The basis for predicting the time when a certain event is likely to occur is the great 120 year planetary cycle which has been popular in Indian astrology. However, it must be mentioned that the method presented here uses the 120 year planetary cycle basis in combination with the constellation ruler and the ninefold progression technique as explained later in the next chapter.

Also, there is another basis, the 108 year planetary cycle which some astrologers use for predicting the time of an event. But our subsequent discussion is based only on the 120 year planetary cycle.

The basic assumption of the great planetary cycle is that the conventional nine planets (Sun, Moon, Mars,

Mercury, Jupiter, Venus, Saturn, Rahu, and Ketu) influence an individual only during their respective cycles. Notice that the modern planets Pluto, Neptune, and Uranus are excluded from the list. There are two reasons. First, the modern planets were not known to astrologers more than three thousand years ago when this system is believed to have been invented. Second, which in my opinion is a more rational reason, the modern planets are so far away from the Earth that their influence on an individual as far as the application of the planetary cycle is concerned is insignificant. Usually they transmit their energy through the planets they are associated with, either through angles or affection. However, according to the K.P. system as discussed later, the influence of the modern planets is realized during the cycles of their respective constellations rulers.

Each of the nine conventional planets as mentioned above is assigned a certain number as years for its major cycle and in a certain sequence as follows.

Ketu	7 years
Venus	20 years
Sun	6 years
Moon	10 years
Mars	7 years
Rahu	18 years
Jupiter	16 years
Saturn	19 years
Mercury	17 years
	120 years

Thus, Ketu's major cycle is 7 years and that of Jupiter is 16 years. Further a major cycle is divided to provide nine intermediate cycles which begin with the major cycle planet, and the duration of the intermediate cycles of the respective planets are proportional to their major cycle years. Thus, as an example under Moon's major cycle, the intermediate cycles are:

Moon	10 months
Mars	7 months
Rahu	18 months
Jupiter	16 months
Saturn	19 months
Mercury	17 months
Ketu	7 months
Venus	20 months
Sun	6 months
	120 months or 10 years

Furthermore, an intermediate cycle of a planet consists of nine sub-cycles. The duration of each of the sub-cycles is proportional to its major cycle year, and the first sub-cycle begins with the intermediate cycle ruler. Thus, under the Moon's major cycle the intermediate cycle of Venus consists of the nine sub-cycles as follow:

Venus	3 months 10 days
Sun	1 month
Moon	1 month 20 days
Mars	1 month 5 days
Rahu	3 months
Jupiter	2 months 20 days
Saturn	3 months 5 days
Mercury	2 months 25 days
Ketu	1 month 5 days
	20 months

There is a total of 729 sub-cycles, eighty one per every major cycle.

These major cycle rulers correspond to the zodiac divisions referred to as the constellations. According to the system employed here, the **fixed** zodiac is distributed over twenty-seven equal length constellations of 13° - 20' zodiac band each. The first, tenth, and the nineteenth constellations which correspond to the first 13° - 20' of Aries, Leo, and Sagittarius are assigned to Ketu. In other words, the first 13° - 20' of Aries, Leo, and Sagittarius are ruled by Ketu.

Similarly, the next successive constellations, 13° - 21' through 26° - 40' of the same three zodiac signs are ruled by the planet Venus; the ninth, eighteenth, and the twenty-seventh constellations which correspond to the last 13° - 20' of Cancer, Scorpio, and Pisces (namely the zone from 16° - 40' to 30° - 00') are assigned to Mercury as their ruler. The following table lists the twenty-seven constellations of the zodiac and their rulers.

Rulers	Constellations	Constellations	Constellations
Ketu	Aries 0° - 13°:20'	Leo 0° - 13°:20'	Sagittarius 0° - 13°:20'
Venus	Aries 13°:20' - 26°:40'	Leo 13°:20' - 26°:40'	Sagittarius 13°:20' - 26°:40'
Sun	Aries 26°:40' - Taurus 10°	Leo 26°:40' - Virgo 10°	Sagittarius 26°:40'-Capricorn 10°
Moon	Taurus 10° - 23°:20'	Virgo 10° - 23°:20'	Capricorn 10° - 23°:20'
Mars	Taurus 23°:20' - Gemini 6°:40'	Virgo 23°:20' - Libra 6°:40'	Capricorn 23°:20'-Aquarius 6°:40'
Rahu	Gemini 6°:40'- 20°	Libra 6°:40' - 20°	Aquarius 6°:40' - 20°
Jupiter	Gemini 20° - Cancer 3°:20'	Libra 20° - Scorpio 3°:20'	Aquarius 20° - Pisces 3°:20'
Saturn	Cancer 3°:20' - 16°:40'	Scorpio 3°:20' - 16°:40'	Pisces 3°:20' - 16°:40'
Mercury	Cancer 16°:40' - 30°	Scorpio 16°:40' - 30°	Pisces 16°:40' - 30°

For a given natal chart, the major, the intermediate, and the sub-cycles that were operative at the time of birth are determined based on the Moon's zodiac position at the time of birth. From Mr. Nixon's natal chart clearly at the time of his birth Mars's major cycle was operative since Moon was placed at 27° - 33' of Capricorn, and the constellation corresponding to the zone from 23° - 20' of Capricorn to 6° - 40' of Aquarius is ruled by Mars. At the time of his birth, Moon was placed at 4° - 13' away from the beginning of the Mars constellation. In other words, Moon was 9° - 7' or 547' away before it could reach the end of Mars's constellation. Therefore, the balance or the remaining duration of Mars's major cycle at his birth time was (547 / 800 x 7) years or 4 years 9 months and 13 days. In other words, 2 years 2 months and 17 days of the Mars's major cycle were passed at the time of Mr. Nixon's birth. Consequently, the intermediate cycle at the time of his birth corresponds to that of Jupiter which begins 1 year 5 months and 15 days after the start of Mars's major cycle and ends after 2 years 4 months and 21 days. Similarly further computation yields the sub-cycle of Mars.

The major cycles and the corresponding dates (or duration) according to Mr. Nixon's natal chart are as follows.

Major Cycle Rulers	Cycle Duration	Starts on	Ends on
Mars	4 Years 9 Mo. 13 Days	January 10, 1913	October 23, 1917
Rahu	18 Years	October 23, 1917	October 23, 1935
Jupiter	16 Years	October 23, 1935	October 23, 1951
Saturn	19 Years	October 23, 1951	October 23, 1970
Mercury	17 Years	October 23, 1970	October 23, 1987
Ketu	7 Years	October 23, 1987	October 23, 1994
Venus	20 Years	October 23, 1994	October 23, 2014

Although the great 120 year cycle concept has been popular in India for over three thousand years, the degree of success achieved by applying this concept is not always satisfactory. In some cases it seems to work well while in others it seems to fail. About sixty years ago, a well known astrologer, Mr. Krishnamurthy from the southern part of India, experimented with the traditional method using hundreds of thousands of horoscopes and modified the way the great 120 year cycle was applied. His modified approach of the constellation ruler concept has come to be known as the K.P. (Krishnamurthy Paddhati) system.

The K.P. system has been very popular since then. I was exposed to it in the late sixties. I experimented with it extensively by applying it to almost every horoscope. However, while it did appear to work better than the traditional approach, there were still some cases where neither of these approaches would yield a satisfactory result. I tried a few variations of the K.P. system on my own, but they did not prove satisfactory either. I continued my pursuit of an approach for improving the prediction of timing an event that would apply to most of the cases. It was not until the early nineties that I accidentally discovered a new approach that blends the concepts of a ninefold horoscope progression, the constellation rulers of the popular K.P. system, and the great 120 year planetary cycles. What follows are the procedural details that will lead you to understand my approach in applying time to the prediction of an event with a fair degree of success.

According to the traditional approach the influence of a planet that affects matters related to the house it occupies and the zodiac sign it belongs to is typically materialized during that planet's major or intermediate or sub-cycle. For instance, in Mr. Nixon's natal chart, the ascendant ruler Sun is in the fifth house occupying the zodiac sign Sagittarius. Then during the Sun's cycle, either intermediate or short (note as per Mr. Nixon's natal chart, the Sun's major cycle doesn't begin until the year 2014), the events related to the first house (health, his temperament, the challenges, the major breaks, fame and prosperity, etc.) and the fifth house (education, children, pursuit of pleasures, entertainment, etc.) matters were expected to occur.

As mentioned earlier, the K.P. system is based on the planetary constellations and the relationship between the planets and the houses they signify.

For example, in Mr. Nixon's horoscope, the ascendant is occupied by Ketu. The constellations that are ruled by Ketu are 0° to 13° - 20' zodiac sign portions of Aries, Leo, and Sagittarius. The planets that occupy any of these zodiac portions are referred to as the planets that occupy Ketu's constellations. There are no planets in the zodiac signs Aries and Leo. The zodiac sign Sagittarius, however, has three planets: Mars (7° - 12'), Mercury (7° - 28'), and Jupiter (9° - 23') that lie in the constellation band (0° to 13° - 20' of Sagittarius) ruled by Ketu.

Next, the ascendant cusp (Leo 24° - 45') is ruled by the sign owner Sun, and the planets that occupy the Sun's constellations are Sun (Sagittarius 26° - 51') and Saturn (Taurus 4° - 57'). According to the K.P. system, therefore, the planets that are responsible for influencing the first house matters are Ketu, Mars, Mercury, Jupiter, Sun, and Saturn. These planets are referred to as the first house signifiers.

Similarly, for each house its signifiers can be determined. The following table summarizes the results. At the bottom of the table, the planets are listed with the houses they signify as a cross reference.

House Number	Occupants	Planets in the Constellations of Occupants	Cusp Sign Ruler	Planets in the Constellations of the Cusp Sign Ruler
I	Ketu	Mars, Mercury, Jupiter	Sun	Sun, Saturn
II			Mercury	
III			Venus	
IV	Mars Mercury Jupiter	Moon, Pluto Neptune	Mars	Moon, Pluto
V	Sun Uranus	Sun, Saturn	Jupiter	Neptune
VI	Moon Venus	Uranus, Ketu	Saturn	Rahu
VII	Rahu	Venus	Saturn	Rahu
VIII			Jupiter	Neptune
IX	Saturn	Rahu	Mars	Moon, Pluto
X	Pluto		Venus	
XI	Neptune		Mercury	
XII			Moon	Uranus, Ketu

Sun	I, I, V, V
Moon	IV, IV, VI, IX, XII
Mars	I, IV, IV, IX
Mercury	I, II, IV, XI
Jupiter	I, IV, V, VIII
Venus	III, VI, VII, X
Saturn	I, V, VI, VII, IX
Uranus	V, VI, XII
Neptune	IV, V, VIII, XI
Pluto	IV, IV, IX, X
Rahu	VI, VII, VII, IX
Ketu	I, VI, XII

Note if a planet signifies the same house more than once by virtue of its occupancy, ruling the house cusp, or occupying the constellations of the occupants and cusp sign ruler, the house is listed in the table that many times. For instance, Sun signifies the first house twice and also the fifth house twice.

In my opinion, the essence of the K.P. system lies in the realization of a prediction due to a certain planet's occurrence not during the cycle of that planet but during the cycle of its constellation ruler, unless either that planet is in its own constellation or there are no planets that belong to the constellations ruled by the planet whose cycle is in operation. This was one of the most brilliant contributions of the K.P. system to modern Indian astrology. In addition, it allows us to include the influence of the modern planets Uranus, Neptune, and Pluto during the cycles of their respective constellation rulers.

In order to illustrate the concept, we must consider a few events in Mr. Nixon's political life.

- He was nominated for Vice President of the United States by the Republican National Convention in 1952 and elected with President Eisenhower in November 1952.

The cycles that were operating during the period of September 15, 1952 through November 21, 1952 were Major-Saturn, Intermediate-Saturn, and Sub-Ketu.

According to the traditional approach Saturn and Ketu should influence the above period. But in the natal chart these planets are not strong enough to warrant Mr. Nixon the political gain of the vice presidency. However, by applying the K.P. system instead, in Mr. Nixon's natal chart Rahu is the only planet in the constellations ruled by Saturn. Mars, Mercury, and Jupiter are in the constellation ruled by Ketu. Remember, Rahu, as discussed in the previous chapter "The Ninefold Horoscope," is the most powerful planet in his horoscope. Being on the ninefold chart ascendant cusp, Rahu helped him realize his political ambition. In addition, Mars, Mercury, and Jupiter aspect the tenth house (the house of profession). Also, being in the direct opposition to the tenth house Pluto, they provided all the support to Pluto's activities. As a matter of fact, it was at the beginning of Saturn's 19 year major cycle (starting October 22, 1951) that his political career began—Rahu's prominent influence operated during the entire 19 year major cycle.

- He was nominated by the Republican Party in 1960 for President of the United States, but lost to President Kennedy in a very tight race.

The cycles that were operating between August 25, 1960 and February 26, 1961 were Major-Saturn, Intermediate-Venus, Sub-Saturn.

During this period, Rahu, being in the constellation of Saturn, was definitely a very positive influence on his gaining the Republican Party nomination. However, since none of the planets belong to any one of the constellations ruled by Venus, and Venus being the weak and inauspicious sixth house occupant in his horoscope, Rahu alone couldn't promise him the victory over his opponent. Later, in the ninefold horoscope progression analysis, this point will be revisited.

- He was again nominated by the Republican Party for President of the United States on August 7, 1968; he was elected President on November 5, 1968.

The cycles that were operating on August 7, 1968 were Major-Saturn, Intermediate-Jupiter, Sub-Jupiter; and on November 5, 1968 the operating cycles were Major-Saturn, Intermediate-Jupiter, Sub-Saturn.

In this case he had excellent support from Rahu and Neptune (Neptune being in the constellation of Jupiter), as both are extraordinarily powerful in his chart. In general, Saturn, Jupiter, and the Sun's cycles were very positive and fruitful for him. Ketu, Mercury, and Moon's cycles were neutral. Rahu, Venus, and Mars's cycles were very negative and destructive.

- He was reelected President of the United States in November 1972.

The cycles that were operating between November 3, 1972 and March 20, 1973 were Major-Mercury, Intermediate-Mercury, Sub-Saturn.

During this period, Rahu again being in the Saturn's constellation guaranteed Mr. Nixon his reelection to the Presidency of the United States.

- He resigned the Presidency on August 9, 1974 after having gone through a very difficult period for about a year.

The cycles that were operating between March 17, 1974 and September 7, 1974 were Major-Mercury, Intermediate-Venus, Sub-Venus.

Since there are no planets in the constellations ruled by either Mercury or Venus, and since both Mercury and Venus are not so powerful in Mr. Nixon's natal chart, this particular cycle was not positive for him. In particular, the adversely placed sixth house Venus in his natal chart brought him down.

11. The Ninefold Progression

In the ninth chapter, using Mr. Nixon's natal chart as an example, the procedure for generating the ninefold horoscope of a natal chart is illustrated. In this chapter, the application of the ninefold horoscope is extended to include planetary progression. The ascendant of the ninefold horoscope of the natal chart is the basis for the ninefold progressive horoscope. Thus, the ascendant for Mr. Nixon's ninefold progressive horoscope remains Scorpio.

In the tenth chapter, five major political events in Mr. Nixon's life were considered and analyzed. The focus of the analysis was to illustrate the concept of the planetary cycles, the traditional approach of its application, and, further, the invention of the K.P. system by Mr. Krishnamurthy. In this chapter, an attempt is made to analyze the same events by applying the ninefold progression technique.

In applying the ninefold progression technique, my basic assumption is the ascendant always remains the same as that of the ninefold horoscope of the person's natal chart. In Mr. Nixon's case, the first step is to show the planetary transitions at the time of the event under consideration in a chart with Scorpio as its ascendant. This chart may be referred as the progressive chart for a particular event in Mr. Nixon's life. The next step is to determine the ninefold planetary transitions for this progressive chart with the same Scorpio ascendant.

Before we analyze Mr. Nixon's progressive charts, the significance of planetary transitions through the houses in these charts need some mention. It is important to note that the information that follows is intended to be a starting point. There are other considerations that must be taken into account before arriving at a conclusion.

In general, Sun, Mars, Saturn, both lunar nodes Rahu and Ketu, Uranus, and Pluto are considered to be favorable when they transit through the third, sixth, tenth, and the eleventh houses of the progressive charts. The remaining houses are deemed unfavorable. However, a planet that has a strong and positive influence on the individual due to its place in both the natal and the ninefold natal charts is likely to be almost unaffected by its unfavorable house transition in the progressive charts. In the same manner, a planet which is negatively placed in the original natal and the ninefold natal chart may not fully provide its positive results due to its transition in the favorable houses in the progressive charts.

While the effect of Jupiter is considered favorable when it transits through the second, fifth, seventh, ninth, and the eleventh house, the influence of Moon is favorable when it moves through the first, third, sixth, seventh, tenth, and the eleventh. The positive results of Mercury are materialized when it transits through fourth, sixth, eighth, tenth, eleventh, and to some extent the second house of the progressive charts. Venus provides favorable results from all the houses except the sixth, seventh, and tenth. The details of the significance of each of these planets with respect to their transit through all the houses of the progressive charts are as follows.

Sun

First House: Blood pressure, heart condition, poor health, frustration, fear, worry, setbacks, delays, humiliation.

Second House: Loans, expenses, deceit, financial loss, eye problems, worry, differences with relatives.

Third House: Material fulfillment, financial gains, good health, prestige, power, praise, daring, boldness.

Fourth House: Health problems, delays, disappointment, unhappiness, unexpected expenses, family difficulties, botheration.

Fifth House: Poor health, accident, friction with the relatives, problems with boss and upper management, opposition, fear of enemy or opponent, worry.

Sixth House: Improvement in health, mental peace and satisfaction, success, happiness, monetary gains.

Seventh House: Quarrel with spouse, worry, fever, indigestion, intestinal and kidney problems.

Eighth House: Fatigue, fever, illness, sadness, fear, fights, negative surroundings, opposition, difference of opinion, illness in family.

Ninth House: Fear, disappointment, insult, demotion, mental strain, opposition by management.

Tenth House: Success, satisfaction, money, fame, prestige, excellent surroundings, opportunities, high level connections.

Eleventh House: Power, fame, promotion, financial prosperity, business expansions, excellent health.

Twelfth House: Disappointments, vascillation, unhappiness, worries, defeat, expenses.

Moon

Moon is generally favorable when it transits through the first, third, sixth, seventh, tenth, and eleventh house of the progressive charts.

Mars and Ketu

First House: Blood disease, intestinal problems, fire related injuries, cuts, poison, wounds, opposition, frustration, dealings with enemies.

Second House: Loss of money, expenses, deceit, fear of enemy, trouble with law, jealousy, hate, fights, quarrels, failures.

Third House: Power, prestige, happiness, fulfillment of ambitions, success, excellent physical shape.

Fourth House: Problems with friends and relatives, disappointment, unhappiness, family difficulties, poor health, indigestion, bleeding, demotion or loss of power.

Fifth House: Children illness, mental strain, unhappiness, sadness, opposition, fear of enemy, worries, loss of money, anger.

Sixth House: Success in all endeavors, generally very happy, monetary gains, victory over enemies, death of enemies.

Seventh House: Quarrel with spouse, loss of money, mental worries, eye and intestinal problems.

Eighth House: Insult, sufferings, poor health, fear of being poisoned, cuts, bloody wounds, fear of enemies.

Ninth House:	Worries, anxieties, poor health, failures, financial setbacks, travel, opposition from high level people.
Tenth House:	Unfavorable surroundings, wrong doings, hard work and eventual success.
Eleventh House:	Power, fame, financial prosperity, real estate gains, happiness in family.
Twelfth House:	Possibility of being framed, spousal illness, unexpected expenses, worries, eye trouble, leg fracture, women trouble, anxieties.

Mercury

First House:	Unsteadiness, loss of money, fight or serious differences with friends, bad company.
Second House:	Although in general unhappy expect some financial gains.
Third House:	Possibility of creating enemies and fear of enemies, trouble with law.
Fourth House:	Happiness in family, financial gains, good times with friends.
Fifth House:	Problems from children and spouse, fear, dullness.
Sixth House:	Fame, monetary gains, positive accomplishments.
Seventh House:	Quarrels, mental worries, temporary separation from loved ones.
Eighth House:	Success, mission completion, happiness.
Ninth House:	Oppositions, delays, quarrels.
Tenth House:	Mental satisfaction, happiness in family, financial prosperity.
Eleventh House:	New friends, monetary gains, satisfaction, happiness.
Twelfth House:	Failures, insults, loans, poor health.

Venus

First House:	Material happiness, luxury, good sex life.
Second House:	Financial gain, happy family life, good married life.
Third House:	Real estate acquisition or gains, social prestige, popularity, financial gains, pleasures and happiness.
Fourth House:	Material happiness in family, financial gains, good times with friends and own children, real estate and farm house expansions, good food.
Fifth House:	Happiness in family, association of good people, satisfaction, praise, prosperity.
Sixth House:	Worries, anxieties, unhappiness, loans, quarrels, dealing with law and courts, prone to illness.
Seventh House:	Association of bad people, spousal problems and troubles, problems in dealing with the opposite sex, loss of money.
Eighth House:	Financial and real estate gains, social prestige, prosperity, and fame.
Ninth House:	Blessed, company of well wishers, happy married life, good and enjoyable life, fame.
Tenth House:	Unhappiness, oppositions.

Eleventh House: Good sex life, monetary gains, satisfaction, happiness in family.

Twelfth House: Luxurious life, material happiness, sensuous satisfaction.

Jupiter

First House: Loss of money, destruction of wealth, poor health, family problems and troubles, worries, obstructions, tedious journeys, migration.

Second House: Success, power, social prestige, promotions, wealth expansion, happiness from all directions, happiness in family.

Third House: Fear, financial losses, unfavorable times for the relatives, failures, demotions, public humiliation, illness, miserable travels.

Fourth House: Betrayal, unnecessary expenses, separation from relatives and well wishers, frustration, family problems, unhappiness.

Fifth House: Newborn arrival in family, gain of knowledge or degree in education, prosperity, lucky, good fortune, fame, social praise, gain in acquaintances, success, prestige, auspicious, good news, wedding in family.

Sixth House: Serious differences with relatives, fear, anxieties, worries, failures, loss of money, unnecessary expenses, poor health, misery.

Seventh House: Good married and sex life, wedding, financial gains, success, acquisition of a new car, arrival of a baby in family.

Eighth House: Trouble with law, misfortune, loss of wealth, unhappiness, acquiring of a disease, separation from the loved ones, miserable travels, family problems.

Ninth House: Very auspicious, materialization, good fortune, success, happiness, satisfaction, peace of mind, social prestige, fame, popularity, owning a bigger and better house, association with good and religious people, good deeds.

Tenth House: Social downfall, public humiliation, failures, exceptions, professional or business setbacks, family problems, illness of children, hopelessness.

Eleventh House: Prosperity, wealth expansion, happiness, satisfaction, marriage, wedding, arrival of a new baby in family, success, social fame.

Twelfth House: Unhappiness, unnecessary expenses, loss of wealth, loss of real estate, separation from family, poor health.

Saturn and Rahu

First House: Problems, illness in family, children and spouse partition, separation, misery, poverty, unnecessary expenses, illness, fear of enemy, death of a relative, migration.

Second House: Quarrels and fights, misfortune in family, loss of money, unhappiness, dangers, illness.

Third House: Victory over enemies or competitors, prestige, social popularity, happiness, financial gains, success in all endeavors.

Fourth House: Temporary separation from friends, kin, spouse, and children; unfavorable period for the parents, unhappiness, frustration, dangers, misfortunes, bad deeds, bad company and surroundings.

Fifth House: Temporary separation from children, abortion, unnecessary and unanticipated expenses, confusion, pessimism, loss of money, family trouble, false accusations.

Sixth House: Victorious over enemies, financial gains, success, happiness, good times.

Seventh House: Temporary separation from spouse, moving out of house, migration to another country, travel, illness of children or spouse, sickness and disease, arthritis, AIDS.

Eighth House: Possibility of losing everything, unhealthy relationships with friends, relatives, and family members resulting in a very unhappy situation, misery, pessimism, destruction, company of wrong people, obsessive gambling, notorious, death of loved ones.

Ninth House: Harassment from enemies, trouble with law, criminal activity, long travel, unsuccessful endeavors, poor health.

Tenth House: Problems and changes in profession or business or career, demotion, humiliation, victim of false accusations, wrong doings, bad intentions, loss of money.

Eleventh House: Real estate acquisition, good married and sex life, prestige, fame, prosperity, expansion of wealth, promotion, happiness, satisfaction, social recognition, happiness in family, success in everything!

Twelfth House: Dangers, loss of money, erosion of wealth, unhappiness, misery, illness, unwanted quarrels and fights, trouble with law, visit to court room, separation from loved ones and relatives, hate, loss of power and social position, humiliation, travel.

Uranus and Pluto

These are generally favorable when they transit through the third, sixth, tenth, and eleventh houses of the progressive charts.

Neptune

Neptune is generally favorable when it moves through the first, third, fifth, ninth, and eleventh houses of the progressive charts.

Let us now analyze Mr. Nixon's progressive chart as shown in Figure 11.1A for November 3, 1952, 6 p.m. (EST), and its corresponding ninefold progressive chart shown in Figure 11.1B for the following event.

He was nominated for Vice President of the United States by the Republican National Convention in 1952 and elected with President Eisenhower in November 1952.

The cycles that were operating during the period of September 15, 1952 through November 21, 1952 were Major-Saturn, Intermediate-Saturn, Sub-Ketu.

As was noted earlier, according to the traditional approach Saturn and Ketu should influence the above period. But in the natal chart these planets are not strong enough to warrant Mr. Nixon the political gain of the vice presidency. However, by applying the K.P. system instead, in Mr. Nixon's natal chart, Rahu is the only planet in the constellations ruled by Saturn, while Mars, Mercury and Jupiter are in the constellation ruled by Ketu.

Remember that Rahu, as discussed in the ninth chapter "The Ninefold Horoscope," is the most powerful planet in his horoscope. Being on the ninefold chart ascendant cusp, it helped him realize his political ambition. Notice, here in the progressive charts, the transit of Rahu in the third house of the progressive chart and in the tenth house of the ninefold progressive chart. The most powerful planet in Mr. Nixon's natal chart moving through the third and the tenth houses of the progressive and the ninefold progressive charts respectively on

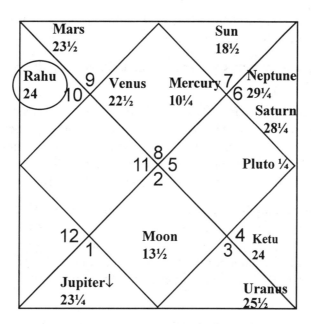

Figure 11.1A: Mr. Nixon's progressive chart for November 3, 1952, 6 p.m.(EST).

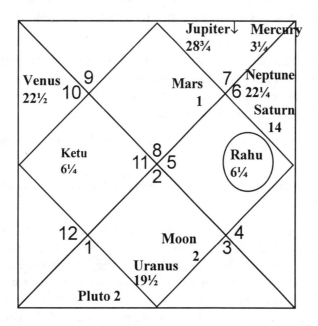

Figure 11.1B: Mr. Nixon's ninefold progressive chart for the above event.

November 3, 1952 assured him the success in the presidential election with President Eisenhower. In addition, note the transit of Pluto and Neptune—Pluto transiting through the tenth and the sixth houses of the progressive charts respectively while Neptune is moving through the eleventh house of both progressive charts has confirmed his success.

The next event is when he was nominated by the Republican Party in 1960 for President of the United States but lost to President Kennedy in a very tight race.

The cycles that were operating between August 25, 1960 and February 26, 1961 were Major-Saturn, Intermediate-Venus, Sub-Saturn.

For this period Rahu, being in the constellation of Saturn, was definitely a very positive factor for him to gain the Republican Party nomination. However, since none of the planets belong to any one of the constellations ruled by Venus, and Venus being the weak and inauspicious sixth house occupant in his horoscope, Rahu alone couldn't promise him the victory over his opponent. Both progressive charts for this event are shown in Figures 11.2A and 11.2B respectively for November 1, 1960, 10 p.m. (EST).

Although Rahu seems to have been well placed in the tenth house of the progressive chart and in the eleventh house of the ninefold progressive chart, it makes a very close square with his most detrimental planet Venus in the progressive chart. It's very interesting to note that he very closely lost to his opponent who probably had a strong and positive Venus in his natal chart. Also, note the poor placing of Saturn, Neptune, Mars, and Jupiter in the progressive chart which might have been responsible for his loss in a tight presidential race.

The third event: Mr. Nixon was again nominated by the Republican Party for President of the United States on August 7, 1968; he was elected President on November 5, 1968.

The cycles that were operating on August 7, 1968 were Major-Saturn, Intermediate-Jupiter, Sub-Jupiter; and on November 5, 1968 they were Major-Saturn, Intermediate-Jupiter, Sub-Saturn.

For this event he had excellent support from Rahu and Neptune (Neptune being in the constellation of Jupiter) as both are extraordinarily powerful in his chart. Both progressive charts and the corresponding ninefold progressive charts for this event are shown in Figures 11.3A and 11.3B respectively for November 5, 1968, 10 p.m. (EST).

Notice the transit of Rahu and Neptune, two of his most positive and the influential planets, through the very favorable houses with the extraordinarily auspicious trine between them in the both progressive charts. In addition, wonderful support from a cluster of five planets transiting through the eleventh house of the progressive chart made it very easy for him to win the presidential election in 1968.

The fourth political event for our analysis is when he was reelected for the office of the Presidency of the United States in November 1972.

The cycles that were operating between November 3, 1972 and March 20, 1973 were Major-Mercury, Intermediate-Mercury, Sub-Saturn.

During this period, again Rahu, being in the Saturn's constellation, continues to help Mr. Nixon to achieve his political ambitions. Since there are no planets in the constellation of Mercury, Rahu is the only planet that has a significant effect on Mr. Nixon during the time of this event. As depicted in Figures 11.4A and 11.4B, in the progressive as well as the corresponding ninefold progressive chart for this event, Rahu is in the second house. In addition, the planet Pluto, which signifies the matter of the tenth house, is in the eleventh house of the progressive chart and in the sixth house of the ninefold progressive chart. Both of these houses are positive and favorable for Pluto. As a result, Mr. Nixon won the election by a landslide. It's also important to note in the progressive chart the transit of Neptune in the favorable first house and that of Uranus in the auspicious

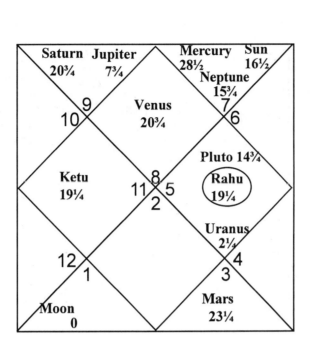

Figure 11.2A: Mr. Nixon's progressive chart for November 1, 1960, 10 p.m. (EST).

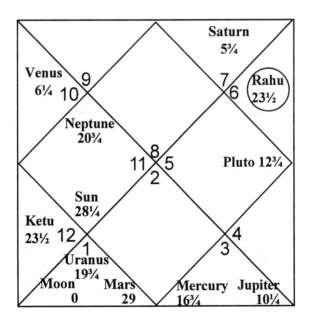

Figure 11.2B: Mr. Nixon's ninefold progressive chart.

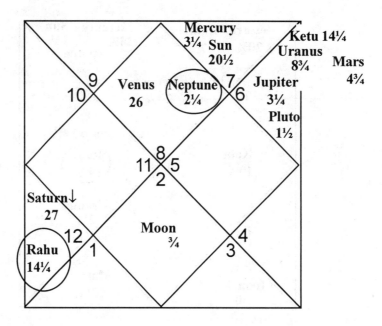

Figure 11.3A: Mr. Nixon's progressive chart for November 5, 1968, 10 p.m. (EST).

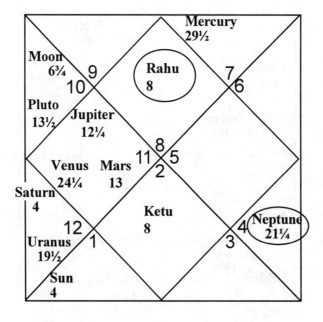

Figure 11.3B: Mr. Nixon's ninefold progressive chart for the above event.

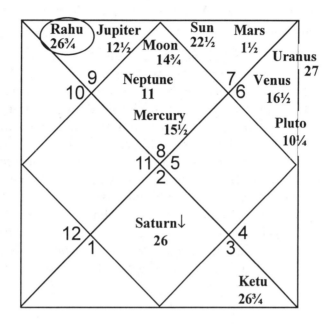

Figure 11.4A: Mr. Nixon's progressive chart for November 7, 1972, 10 p.m. (EST).

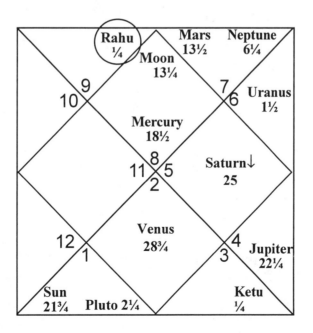

Figure 11.4B: Mr. Nixon's ninefold progressive chart for the above.

eleventh house.

The last event of our analysis is the time when Mr. Nixon resigned the Presidency on August 9, 1974 after having gone through a very difficult period for at least a year.

The cycles that were operating between March 17, 1974 and September 7, 1974 were Major-Mercury, Intermediate-Venus, Sub-Venus.

Since there are no planets in the constellations ruled by either Mercury or Venus, the positive and powerful effect of Rahu was no longer in operation for him during this particular period. In addition, both Mercury and Venus are not so powerful in Mr. Nixon's natal chart. Note the position of Mercury and Venus in the progressive chart shown in Figure 11.5A for August 9, 1974, 10 a.m. (EST). Both were transiting through the politically unfavorable ninth house (ninth house being the twelfth from the tenth) indicating this particular event was definitely not positive for him. Also, note the unfavorable square of Uranus and Venus in both progressive and ninefold charts. Finally, a close observation of the analysis of the progressive and ninefold progressive charts for all the five political events in Mr. Nixon's life clearly proves that only during the cycles through which the period of the positive and powerful planet's influence (in this case Saturn's cycle through which Rahu's period was operative, and Jupiter's cycle through which Neptune's period was operative) was operative, and only with their favorable placement in both the corresponding progressive and ninefold progressive charts, the results signified by those planets are realized. Without the confirmation by the progressive and the ninefold progressive charts, the realization of matters signified by the powerful planets in their operative cycles is not guaranteed!

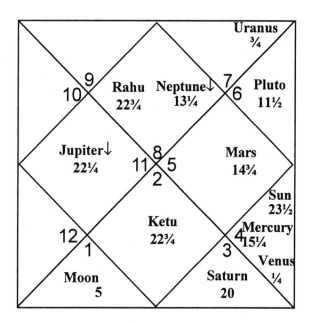

Figure 11.5A: Mr. Nixon's progressive chart for August 9, 1974, 10 a.m. (EST).

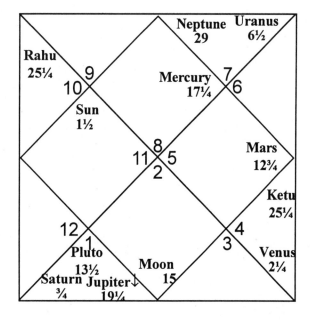

Figure 11.5B: Mr. Nixon's ninefold progressive chart for the above event.

Bibliography

1. Bhat Vasant Damodar, "Kundali-Tantra aani Mantra," Part I and II in Marathi, an Indian language, *Gemini Jyotish Karyalaya*, Prakashan, Pune (India).
2. Kharegat K. M., "Some Little Known Systems of House Divisions, I - XI," *The Astrological Magazine*, April 1971- December 1971, Banglore, India.
3. Krishnamurthy, K. S., "First Reader: Casting the Horoscope," "Second Reader: Fundamental Principles of Astrology," "Third Reader: Predictive Stellar Astrology," "Fourth Reader: Marriage, Married Life, and Children," "Fifth Reader: Horary Astrology-Advanced Stellar System," Mahabala Publishers and Book Sellers, Madras, India (1974).
4. *Raphael's Tables of Houses for Northern Latitudes*, W. Foulsham & Co., Ltd., Yeovil Road, Slough, Bucks., England .
5. Rudhyar Dane, *The Astrology of America's Destiny*, Vintage Books, A Division of Random House, New York, 1975.
6. Rudhyar Dane, *Astrological Timing -The Transition to the New Age*, Harper Colophon Books, New York.
7. Thomas G. Shanks, *The American Atlas*, Expanded Fifth Edition, ACS Publications.
8. *World Ephemeris for the 20th Century, 1900 to 2000 at Greenwich Noon*, Para Research, Rockport, Massachusetts.